IMPROVING PARENT-ADOLESCENT RELATIONSHIPS

LEARNING ACTIVITIES FOR PARENTS AND ADOLESCENTS

LEADER MANUAL

DARRELL J. BURNETT, Ph.D.

ACCELERATED DEVELOPMENT INC.
3808 West Kilgore Avenue
Muncie, IN 47304-4896
Toll Free Order Number 1-800-222-1166

IMPROVING PARENT-ADOLESCENT RELATIONSHIPS
Leader Manual

Copyright 1992 by Accelerated Development Inc.

10   9   8   7   6   5   4   3   2

Printed in the United States of America

Technical Development: Tanya Benn
                         Virginia Cooper
                         Cynthia Long
                         Marguerite Mader
                         Sheila Sheward

ISBN: 1-55959-034-3

Order additional copies from

ACCELERATED DEVELOPMENT INC., PUBLISHERS
3808 West Kilgore Avenue
Muncie, Indiana 47304-4896
Toll Free Order Number 1-800-222-1166

DEDICATION

To my loving wife, Susann,
for her inspiration, encouragement,
typing, and proofreading.
To my wonderful children, Matt, Tom, and Jill,
for their humor, energy, and support.

PREFACE

When I began to develop and gather materials for this program, I was looking for an end product that would be **practical, inexpensive, relevant,** and **applicable** in a wide variety of settings.

The topics covered in this program evolved over a four year period during which I was leading multifamily groups for parents and adolescents in inpatient settings, outpatient clinics, and occasionally for juvenile court diversion programs. Through feedback from parents and adolescents as to which **topics** they felt were most relevant, and which **activities** they felt were most productive. The program eventually evolved into 15 sessions covering three main topic areas: (1) perceiving each other (social perception), (2) communicating effectively, and (3) recognizing behavior as a function of its consequence. The enthusiastic response of participants emphasized these three areas.

The activities involving social perception in the first three sessions received remarks such as the following:

> "It's about time I'm getting my parent to look at the way *I* see things!"

> "I never thought I'd see the day my **kid** would actually try to look at how I see things!"

The effective communication activities received responses such as the following:

> " Thanks to the structured activities, the prepared scripts, and the scoring grid, we were able to stay 'on track'!"

"I liked being able to talk to my parents about negative feelings without all the yelling and screaming that usually goes on."

"The activities really help us talk in a civil manner to each other on touchy subjects."

"I've never tried to 'get into my parent's shoes' before. What a trip!"

"When we did those empathy activities, I couldn't believe it. There we were, actually focusing on each others' thoughts and feelings without getting defensive. A parent's dream! A major breakthrough for us!"

The activities that centered around recognizing behavior as a function of its consequence were extremely well received, with statements such as the following:

"It's great to be able to work on skills, learning to **do** something about our complaints with each other instead of mutual finger pointing."

"I like the 'no fault' approach to problem solving. We used our energy solving instead of blaming."

"The contract activity was something else! I never thought I'd be able to actually sit down and **negotiate** with my parents!"

Besides the topics which evolved, the **approach** used in the program was also determined by the response of the participants. They seemed to prefer the **structured, hands-on, skills training** approach rather than a generalized, unstructured discussion group. Some of their responses were the following:

"The structured activities made the sessions more productive. No one family was able to monopolize the sessions. We all had a chance to learn the materials."

"I like the emphasis on learning **skills** rather than airing our dirty laundry in front of everybody."

The fact that the program involves parents and adolescents participating **together** in each session was a positive feature mentioned repeatedly.

"We didn't have to 'role play' what we **would** say to our parents if they were there. They **were** there! And we got to practice face-to-face with them!"

"Just having our son in the same room practicing the activities with us, made the whole program seem more like a 'family' activity, not an 'us vs. him' situation."

As for the **format** of this Leader Manual, I've tried to make it "user friendly." Each session is spelled out with goals, basic information to be conveyed, and step-by-step procedures, beginning with seating arrangement at the start of the session and ending with the lead-in statement to introduce the next session. The group leader simply has to follow the procedure outlined in this manual, and guide the participants to compete the forms and the activities contained in the Participant Workbook.

Although the program developed in the context of a multifamily group, the materials and sessions work equally well for individual family treatment.

Finally, just as this program evolved over time, it may well continue to develop. Accordingly, if, in the process of using these materials, new applications arise, I would appreciate feedback of ideas for future additions or revisions.

Darrell J. Burnett, Ph.D.

CONTENTS

LIST OF FIGURES

PROGRAM

Overview

Outline for Individual Sessions

Part I

Part II

Part III

OVERVIEW

PURPOSE

The purpose of the parent-adolescent program sessions is to offer a learning experience for parents and adolescents working together to improve their skills in areas which are the foundation for healthy family life:

(1) perceiving each other, (2) communicating effectively, and (3) recognizing behavior as a function of its consequences. The sessions are organized under these three categories.

Perceiving Each Other

The first three sessions dwell on the practical and pertinent topic of perceiving each other, and address the age old "generation gap" experience, helping parents and adolescents to see eye-to-eye. The sessions offer them an opportunity to become aware of how **close** or **far away** they are from each other in the way they perceive each other's **personality traits** (Session 1), in the way they perceive how **communications** are going within the family (Session 2), and in the way they perceive each other's **values** (Session 3).

Through these social perception activities parents and adolescents will learn skills of accurate perception of each other, acknowledging similarities and differences.

Communicating Effectively

The next six sessions dwell on the topic of **assertive communication,** exposing parents and adolescents to the various styles of communication between parents and adolescents, helping them identify and develop assertive **problem-solving** approaches to communications within the family setting. The various topics include **communication styles** (Session 4), distinguishing **assertive, aggressive,** and **passive** problem-solving approaches (Session 5), and effective communication **techniques** while expressing feelings concerning **family issues** (Session 6), **positive feelings** towards family members (Sessions 7), **negative feelings** towards family members (Session 8), and feelings of **empathy** toward family members (Session 9).

The purpose for these sessions is to help parents and adolescents develop the skill of being able to "get the point across" while standing up for one's self, yet recognizing the dignity and point of view of the other family member.

Recognizing Behavior as a Function of Its Consequence

The final six sessions dwell on the topic of understanding why behaviors occur, and learning some **techniques** for changing and/or managing behaviors within the home setting. Topics include **The Law of Effect:** behavior and its relation to **consequences** (Session 10); **developmental** and **behavioral** approaches toward understanding adolescence (Session 11); the **role of parents** in **applying consequences** for behaviors (Session 12); **assessing** how parents apply **negative** consequences: **punishment versus logical and natural consequences** (Session 13); learning to **identify specific behaviors** (Session 14); and setting up a **family behavior contract** (Session 15).

STRUCTURE

The program is organized as a series of 15 **skills training** classes rather than as "rap" groups. Each session involves a specific topic with hands-on paper-pencil activities, active participation, and occasional lectures. Each participant is given a copy of the *Participant Workbook* which contains most of the forms used in the paper-pencil activities. The emphasis is upon learning new skills to improve parent-adolescent relationships rather than on ruminative blaming.

With an emphasis upon a "teaching" format families seem less resistive. The format allays their fears that they will have to "air their dirty laundry" in front of others.

Topics included are general in nature and are presented as part of "family life" issues.

Each session is self contained, but many follow logically from the previous session.

LENGTH OF PROGRAM WORKSHOP

The program consists of 15 sessions, each session lasting approximately 50 to 60 minutes. The sessions are optimally held weekly, allowing for practice of activities between sessions.

LEADER QUALIFICATIONS

The program can be facilitated easily by counselors, pastoral counselors, probation officers, mental health workers, psychologists, or social workers. In the manual are listed step-by-step instructions, with all the necessary figures and references. All forms are supplied in the *Participant Workbook*. Some figures in the *Leader Manual* will need to be reproduced for participants. Permission is given to do so.

FACILITIES NEEDED

A well ventilated, well lit room with tables and chairs is adequate. Ideally, the room will be large enough to separate adolescents on one side and parents on the other during those sessions where they are doing written activities separate from each other.

A chalkboard or easel is a must.

SIZE OF GROUP

The program has been successfully conducted with as many as 25 adolescents and their parents. However, the program also can be used for one single family if desired.

SELECTION OF GROUP PARTICIPANTS

The program is appropriate for any population, ranging from "problem" adolescents in a variety of setting's (inpatient, outpatient, aftercare, juvenile diversion, etc.) to adolescents and families looking to improve what good interactions they already have (church groups, personal enrichment groups, etc.).

COST

To run the workshop the basic cost is a copy of the *Participant Workbook* for each participant (adolescents and parents) and a copy of the *Leader Manual* for the leader.

The leader will need access to a copier for duplicating extra figures as needed in some of the sessions.

The leader also should keep a supply of pencils available.

The leader will need an audio tape recorder for Session 4, "Communication Styles," if the audio tape is used. This is not essential. An alternate plan is to role-play the scripts.

Part I

PERCEIVING
EACH OTHER

PERSONALITY TRAITS

GOALS

1. To enable parents and adolescents to better understand their perception of one another's personality traits.

2. To enable parents and adolescents to recognize how close or how far apart they are in their perceptions.

INFORMATION

The first session deals with the topic of how **close** or how **far away** parents and adolescents are from each other in their perception of **personality traits** of each other.

Emphasize the following points:

- Social perception, how people perceive others, is a key to understanding how family members interact with each other.

- Social perception, how we see each other, should be based upon **actual current** behaviors (within the previous six months).

- In many families, parents and adolescents "hold on" to old views of each other regardless of current behavior changes. Thus, dad or mom may be seen as "cruel and mean" because of an incident from two years ago, regardless of changes since then and regardless of the absence of any "cruel and mean" behaviors in the past two years. Likewise, an adolescent may be seen as "selfish and ungiving" because of an incident two years ago, regardless of changes since then and regardless of the absence of "selfish and ungiving" behavior during the last two years.

PROCEDURES

1. Separate parents from their adolescents. Adolescents sit on one side of the room, parents on the other side.

2. Call their attention to the one page description of "Social Perception: Its Effect on Family Communication" found in the *Participant Workbook*. Emphasize the points mentioned under "Information" concerning the connection between social perception and behavior among family members.

3. Explain that this Session and Sessions 2 and 3 will be centered around **social perception** activities among family members covering the topics of **personality traits** (this session), **communicating** within the family (Session 2), and **values held** (Session 3).

4. Instruct parents to complete the "Family Social Perception: Parent Form" (Form 1 in the *Participant Workbook*). Father and mother each complete the form separately (no peeking!).

5. At the same time, instruct the adolescents to complete the "Family Social Perception: Adolescent Form" (Form 2 in the *Participant Workbook*). If the family has two or more children, each child completes his or her own form (no peeking!).

6. Instruct all participants (parents and adolescents) to each fill out *all 10* spaces for each category.

7. Instruct them to be **specific** in their description, and to describe **personality traits,** *not* physical appearances (i.e., "Five foot two, eyes of blue").

8. Remind them to write **current** descriptions, mentally noting a **current** behavioral example for each descriptor.

9. Allow 20 to 25 minutes for completion of the forms.

10. Direct parents and adolescents to sit together to compare forms. Instruct them as they review each other's answers, to give **specific** examples for each description on the form. Thus, if an adolescent describes mom as "cold and calculating," he/she must give a **current** (last six months) example of that behavior. (**NOTE:** This discussion takes place privately among the members of each family, not as a demonstration for all group members.)

11. After 15 or 20 minutes of discussion between parents and adolescents, poll the group concerning the number of **positive** descriptions versus negative descriptions on Parts A, B, and C as described in Numbers 12 and 13.

12. Poll the adolescents (show of hands) asking:

    How many of you had more **negatives** than positives on Part A, "How I Describe Myself "?

    How many of you had more **positives** than negatives on Part A, "How I Describe Myself " ?

    (Use this same format for Parts B and C. Record all responses on the chalkboard.)

13. Poll the parents (show of hands) in the same way, covering Parts A through C. Record all responses on the chalkboard.

14. Discuss the significance of an **overemphasis** upon positives or negatives in social perception.

    For example, if an **adolescent** describes himself or herself (Part A) in mainly **positive** descriptors, but describes his or her parents (Part B) in mainly **negative** descriptors, and expects negative descriptors from the parents (Part C), this is the profile of a teen who tends to **blame** all problems on the parents. Likewise, if a **parent** describes himself or herself (Part A) in mainly **positive** descriptors, but describes the teenager (Part B) in mainly **negative** descriptors, and expects **negative** descriptors from the teenager (Part C) this is the profile of a parent who **blames** all the problems on the teenager.

In another example, if the **adolescent** describes himself or herself (Part A) in mainly **negative** descriptors but describes parents (Part B) in mainly **positive** descriptors, and expects **positive** descriptors from parents (Part C), this may be the profile of a **depressed** teenager who feels his or her parents **don't really know** or are unwilling to look at the negative aspects of their son or daughter.

15. Discuss the importance of trying to develop a **realistic** balance of social perceptions within the family, acknowledging both the positive and negative aspects of each family member, attempting to **increase** the positives while acknowledging the negatives.

16. Poll the families concerning whether, overall, they felt they agreed or disagreed with each other on the various descriptors in the three parts, and whether there were any surprises.

17. Discuss the importance of giving **specific** examples in areas of disagreement. That is, if dad describes himself as "warm and wonderful," but the teenager describes dad as "cold and calculating," they should each be able to cite **current** examples.

18. Briefly discuss Parts D and E, concerning friends.

    a. Ask parents to discuss how they arrive at their perceptions (positive or negative) of their teenager's friends (clothes, hair, makeup, music, language, etc.).

    b. Ask teenagers to discuss how they form their perceptions (positive or negative) of peers in terms of whether they want them for friends.

19. Conclude the session with a reminder that it is very important to keep perceptions **current** and to be willing to change "old" views of each other within the family.

20. Remind the group that the next session will continue the topic of social perception, but with an emphasis upon how they see family **communication.**

SOCIAL PERCEPTION

ITS EFFECT ON FAMILY COMMUNICATION

When family members communicate with each other, their **behavior communicates how they see themselves,** but, more important, it communicates how they see the **others.** For example, if family members perceive another family member as an unworthy person, their behavior toward that family member may communicate rejection. Self-perception and the perception of others become central in understanding family communication in general, and communication in maltreating families in particular.

A **person's behavior at any given moment is influenced by that person's current perceptions of self and other** and by previously acquired and reinforced patterns of communication with the other person. Thus, in order to understand a family's interaction patterns, we need to understand how the family members view themselves and each other; we also need to understand how the perception of self and others interacts with the previously developed patterns of communication and with general personal characteristics of family members' to create altogether unique patterns of interaction and mutual behaviors.

COMMUNICATING WITHIN THE FAMILY

GOALS

1. To enable parents and adolescents to understand better their perceptions of one another's communication patterns in the family.

2. To enable parents and adolescents to recognize how close or how far apart they are in their perceptions.

INFORMATION

This second session deals with the topic of how **close** or how **far away** parents and adolescents are from each other in their perception of **communications** within the family setting.

Emphasize the following points:

- The purpose of the exercise is to help both parents and adolescents to become more **aware** of any differences in perception concerning communications, based upon **actual current behaviors.**

- **Communication** problems are cited most frequently when families are asked to list **major** problem areas when children reach their adolescent years.

PROCEDURES

1. Separate parents from their adolescents, each sitting on a separate side of the room.

2. Remind parents and adolescents of the importance of social perception in family life (give a brief recap from Session 1).

3. Have parents complete Form 3, "Communication Questionnaire for the Parents" (copy is in the *Participant Workbook*) as it applies to their own family. Father and mother each complete a questionnaire separately. Have extra copies available to hand out if necessary.

4. At the same time, have adolescents complete Form 4, "Communication Questionnaire for the Adolescent" (copy is in the *Participant Workbook*) from the adolescent's point of view. If two or more adolescents from the same family are present, each completes the questionnaire separately. Have extra copies available to hand out if necessary.

5. Allow 5 to 10 minutes, reminding all participants to fill in the sentences on Numbers 23 through 26 of the questionnaire.

6. After they have completed the "Questionnaires," while they are still sitting apart from each other, ask the parents and adolescents to try to "get into each other's shoes."

7. Call attention to Item 26 on the **adolescent questionnaire,** and read aloud "Most parents don't realize that . . ." Ask the parents to "put themselves in their adolescent's shoes," completing the statement as they think their adolescent completed it. Responses are to be given orally, but the leader writes them on the chalkboard.

8. After each parent has ventured a guess, ask the adolescents to read their answers individually. Record them on the chalkboard.

9. Briefly discuss any differences of opinion. (**NOTE:** The "generation gap" is often mentioned. This offers an opportunity to discuss the pressures of adolescence today as compared with the previous generation.)

10. Utilizing Item 26 on the *parent questionnaire,* read aloud "Most adolescents don't realize that . . ." and ask the adolescents to "put themselves in their parents' shoes." Ask them to complete the statement as they think their parents completed it. Responses are to be given orally, but the leader records them on the chalkboard.

11. After each adolescent has ventured a guess, ask the parents to read their answers, recording them on the chalkboard.

12. Briefly discuss any differences of opinion.

13. Direct parents and adolescents to now sit *together* and compare their responses on the various items on the questionnaire. Allow approximately 15 minutes.

14. While they are reviewing the items with each other, emphasize to both parents and adolescents that, as they review the questionnaires, each member of the family should have *specific examples* to back up his or her responses to the questionnaire. Thus, if a parent answers, "almost always" to the question "do you listen to your adolescent?", the parent should be able to cite *repeated recent* examples of how he or she "listened" to his or her adolescent. Likewise, if an adolescent answers "almost always" to the question "do your parents interrupt you?", the adolescent should be able to cite *repeated recent* examples of this behavior in the parent.

15. Conclude the session by once again emphasizing the need to base social perception on *actual current behaviors* over the past six months.

16. Remind the group that the next session will continue social perception activities, but will cover the topic of *values,* allowing each family member to compare values with each other.

VALUES

GOALS

1. To enable parents and adolescents to better understand their perception of one another's values.

2. To enable parents and adolescents to recognize how close or how far apart they are in their perception of each other's values.

INFORMATION

This third session deals with the perception and discussion of values within the family.

Emphasize the following points:

- The purpose of the exercise is to help both the parent and the adolescent become aware of how **close** or how **far apart** they are when it comes to their perception of each other in terms of their **values.**

- Families need to discuss values with each other and to discuss how they arrived at **choosing** those values.

- Values are shown by **action** and **behavior,** not by talk.

- Parents need to be careful of living a **double standard** with their teenagers, following the "do as I say, not as I do" standard.

PROCEDURES

1. Separate parents from their adolescents. Adolescents sit on one side of the room, parents on the other side.

2. Briefly recap the topic of the importance of social perception in family interaction (as done in Sessions 1 and 2).

3. Introduce the topic of "values" by noting the traditional "generation gap" phenomenon which has been in recorded history for centuries. Note that, with the rapid pace of change in technology, science, and communications, it seems more and more difficult for parents to presume that their adolescents are experiencing life in the same way as they did in their teens.

4. Emphasize that this session offers an opportunity to see just how similar, or different, parents and adolescents are in terms of standard values.

5. Have parents complete Form 5, "Values: Parent Questionnaire" (copy is in the *Participant Workbook*). Father and mother each complete separate questionnaires. Have extra copies available to hand out if necessary.

6. At the same time, have the adolescents complete Form 6, "Values: Adolescent Questionnaire" (copy is in the *Participant Workbook*). If two or more adolescents are from the same family, each completes a separate questionnaire. Have extra copies available to hand out if necessary.

7. Make sure that all participants understand that, in the ranking of **values** and **personality traits**, they may only use each ranking number **once.** That is, they must pick the **single value** which they rank highest, and score it with a "1." They must then pick the single value which they rank second highest, and score it with a "2", and so on. Thus, on the top half of the questionnaire they must use the numbers 1 through 10, each value having a **separate** number. On the bottom half of the questionnaire, where they rank **personality traits,** they

must use the numbers 1 through 8, each trait having a separate number.

8. Remind parents to predict the three values and three personality traits from the list which they feel their adolescent will list as most important.

9. Remind adolescents to predict three values and three personality traits from the list which they think their parents (mom and/or dad) will list as most important.

10. Make sure everyone understands what each item means. (Thus, "salvation" refers to **religion** as a value; "recognition of other" refers to **being noticed by others** as a value, etc.)

11. Allow 10 to 15 minutes for completion of the questionnaire.

12. Poll the adolescents concerning their **top two** responses on the **values** listed on the top half of the questionnaire. Ask for a show of hands and proceed as follows: "How many scored 'Equality' with a 1 or a 2?", "How many scored 'Family Life' with a 1 or a 2?" (continue through the list down to and including "salvation"). Record the responses on the chalkboard.

13. Poll the parents concerning their top two responses on the same list of **values.** Record on the chalkboard.

14. Poll the adolescents concerning their top two responses (show of hands) on the **personality traits** listed on the bottom half of the questionnaire as follows: "How many scored 'caring' with a 1 or a 2?", "How many scored "creative" with a 1 or 2?" (continue through the list down to and including "truthful"). Record on the chalkboard.

15. Briefly discuss the difference between a "value," which is shown through **action** and an "ideal," which may or may not be shown through action.

16. Use "family life" as an example, and discuss how an adolescent shows through his/her behaviors that family life is a value to him/her.

17. Ask group members for **sample** behaviors which show that family life is important to an **adolescent** (family activities, family chores, family meals, respect for family property, etc.).

    (**NOTE:** If the workshop is in an inpatient hospital setting, examples from hospitalization can be used: civil communications during visits or phone calls; less demanding remarks and more requesting; active participation in family therapy and family groups; family involvement while on family pass; etc.)

18. Ask the group members for sample behaviors which show that family life is important to **parents** (family activities, family support, family meals, time with family, etc.).

    (**NOTE:** If this is a group in an inpatient hospital setting, examples from hospitalization can be used: decision to hospitalize; civil communications during visits and phone calls; active participation in family therapy, family groups, and family passes, etc.)

19. Discuss the difficulties in making time for family life due to work schedules, school activities, etc.

20. Discuss "caring" as an example of a personality trait and discuss how an **adolescent** shows, by his or her behavior, that "caring" is a valued personality trait. Ask for examples of adolescent "caring" behaviors. Ask parents how their adolescents show "caring" behaviors in the family (respect, listening, physical hugs, communicating, accountability for whereabouts, observation of reasonable curfew, etc.).

21. Discuss how a **parent** shows, by his or her behavior, that "caring" is a valued personality trait. Ask for examples of a how a parent shows that he or she cares for the family (economic support, moral support, listening, communicating). Ask this question: "Does a parent show he or she cares for his or her adolescent by **setting limits**?" Emphasize that parents are liable for their children legally until age 18, and that setting limits may be their way

of caring for their adolescent who needs guidance on the way to independence.

22. Instruct parents and adolescents to sit together to compare their lists of ranked values and personality traits, noting similarities and differences.

23. Allow 10 minutes for comparison and discussion among the family members. (**NOTE:** This is done *privately,* not as a demonstration for the rest of the group.)

24. Conclude by reminding parents and adolescents to continue to be aware of whether their *actions* back up what they say their *values* are. Encourage them to practice behaviors which reflect "family life" and "caring" as prime values.

25. At the end of the session summarize how these three sessions have emphasized social perception, enabling parents and adolescents to see how close or how far away they are in how they see each other. Encourage them to keep their perceptions based upon *current* behaviors, updating them every six months.

26. Introduce Part II by stating that the next six sessions will center around a new topic: *communications.* Inform them that Session 4 will examine four basic communication *styles* between adolescents and their parents.

Part II

COMMUNICATING EFFECTIVELY

COMMUNICATION STYLES

GOALS

1. To help parents and adolescents identify and develop an assertive communication style within the family setting.

2. To help parents and adolescents learn to identify four basic styles of communication between parents and adolescents: authoritarian, inconsistent, overprotective, and problem-oriented styles.

INFORMATION

Session 4 deals with four ways that parents and adolescents can communicate with each other. During this session, parents and adolescents listen to four scenarios or scripts depicting distinct communication styles. These styles may either be recorded onto an audiotape before the session, role-played during the session (the preferred way), or read aloud during the session.

Emphasize the following points:

- As these styles are depicted, families may find that several of these styles apply to them.

- *Awareness* of how they communicate with each other is the first step in improving communications.

PROCEDURES

1. Direct the parents and adolescents to sit together and to practice the activity as a *family unit.*

2. Explain the procedure for the session telling them that they will be listening to four (A,B,C and,D) styles of communication between parents and adolescents. Call their attention to Form 7, "Parent-Adolescent Communication Styles: Answer Sheet" (copy is in the *Participant Workbook*). Explain that, as a family unit, they will be asked to listen to each style, and then to answer the four questions concerning each style: (1) What **name** would you give the style?, (2) What are the **strengths** and **weaknesses** of the style?, (3) What was accomplished?, and (4) What are the **feelings** of the parent and the adolescent in each style?

3. Explain that they are to work on **one style at a time.** That is, after listening to Style "A," they are to answer the four questions on the answer sheet pertaining to Style "A."

4. Present Style "A" to the group, either on a pre-recorded audiotape or through role-playing, with a female reading the "mother" script, and a male reading the "son" script. Copy of the script for Style "A" is included in the *Leader Manual* and the *Participant Workbook.* The family members may want to review wording as they answer the four questions.

5. After presenting Style "A," ask the individual families, as individual units, to fill in the four questions for Style "A." Make sure all family members participate in filling out the answer sheet, each family *individually.*

6. After five minutes, poll the families for their responses to the questions, beginning with how they would "name" the style.

7. Record the responses on the chalkboard.

8. After all four questions have been discussed by the families and the responses have been recorded on the chalkboard, hand out Figure 1, "Parent-Adolescent Communication Style A: *Discussion Sheet*" (copy is in the *Leader Manual*). Permission is granted to reproduce sufficient numbers of Figures 1 through 4 to supply each participant with a copy of each figure. **NOTE:** Do **not** hand out the discussion sheet until *after* the families have completed their answer sheet and have discussed their responses concerning the style presented. Each family receives *one* discussion sheet. This encourages them to work together as a unit.

9. Review the items on the discussion sheet. (**NOTE:** Usually, most of the material has already been mentioned by the families in their responses which have been recorded on the chalkboard.)

   An important point to make when discussing the **long-term consequences** for each style is that these are consequences if this particular style is the **predominant** way of communicating. That is, an **occasional** authoritarian approach will not lead to the long term consequence mentioned.

10. Present Style "B."

11. Ask the families, as a unit, to fill in the four questions for Style "B" on the answer sheet.

12. After five minutes poll the families for their responses, recording the responses on chalkboard.

13. Hand out Figure 2, "Parent-Adolescent Communication Style B: *Discussion Sheet*" (copy in the *Leader Manual*).

14. Review the items on the discussion sheet. Emphasize the importance of **consistency** when it comes to family communication. Emphasize the importance of **following through** with promises, positive or negative. Emphasize

(Continued on Page 26)

DIRECTIONS:

1. One copy of Figure 1 is for each family.
2. Work together as a family.
3. Compare responses in your family to those listed for Style A.

ITEMS	RELATION TO STYLE A
1. Name:	Authoritarian
2. Weaknesses:	One sided communciation Parental goal—**strict obedience** "Follow the rules or get out"
3. Accomplishment:	Rules are established
4. Feelings of Mom:	Angry, cold, powerful, domineering
Son:	Powerless, threatened, frustrated, hurt
5. Long term Consequences:	No self-confidence Obey out of fear of punishment Rule by power

Figure 1. Parent-Adolescent Communication Style A Discussion Sheet.*

*Adapted by Darrell J. Burnett, Ph.D., with permission from Brownstone, J.E., and Dye, C.J. (1973). *Communication Workshop for Parents of Adolescents: Leader's Guide.* Champaign, IL: Research Press.

**Permission is granted to reproduce sufficient number of this figure to supply each participant with a copy.

DIRECTIONS:

1. One copy of Figure 2 is for each family.
2. Work together as a family.
3. Compare responses in your family to those listed for Style B.

ITEMS	RELATION TO STYLE B
1. Name:	Inconsistent
2. Weaknesses:	Inconsistent application of consequences Parental goal—**avoid conflict** at any cost Mom "gives in" Son is sarcastic
3. Accomplishment:	Manipulation: Son got mother to clean room
4. Feelings of Mom:	"Martyr," overwhelmed, "poor me"
Son:	Resistant, until mom "gives in" No empathy
5. Long term Consequences:	Trouble with authority Manipulation Irriational reactions Egocentric

Figure 2. Parent-Adolescent Communication Style B
Discussion Sheet.*

*Adapted by Darrell J. Burnett, Ph.D., with permission from Brownstone, J.E., and Dye, C.J. (1973). *Communication Workshop for Parents of Adolescents: Leader's Guide.* Champaign, IL: Research Press.

to parents the importance of presenting a *"united front"* when communicating with teens, otherwise teens will spend most of the time trying to "split" the parents on issues of discipline.

15. Present Style "C."

16. Ask the families, as a unit, to fill in the four questions for Style "C" on the answer sheet.

17. After five minutes poll the families for their responses, recording the responses on the chalkboard.

18. Hand out Figure 3, "Parent-Adolescent Communication Style C: *Discussion Sheet*" (found in *Leader Manual*).

19. Review the items on the discussion sheet. Emphasize the improvement of communication in Style "C," with more *two-way conversation* than in the previous two styles. Emphasize the danger of overdoing *guilt* and need for other's *approval* as the main motivators when parents communicate with adolescents.

20. Present Style "D."

21. Ask the family, as a unit, to fill in the four questions for Style "D" on the answer sheet.

22. After five minutes poll the families for their responses, recording the responses on the chalkboard.

23. Hand out Figure 4, "Parent-Adolescent Communication Style D: *Discussion Sheet*" (found in the *Leader Manual*).

24. Review the items on the discussion sheet. Emphasize that the problem-oriented style of communication with its *two-way conversation* and emphasis upon *mutual problem solving* is the ideal form of family communication and is the goal for families to reach.

25. Emphasize that this style requires *maturity* in that both sides have to admit that they are part of the communication problem.

(Continued on Page 29)

DIRECTIONS:

1. One copy of Figure 3 is for each family.
2. Work together as a family.
3. Compare responses in your family to those listed for Style C.

ITEMS	RELATION TO STYLE C
1. Name:	Overprotective
2. Weaknesses:	Parental goal—Get daughter to use "approval of others" as her reason for behavior Guilt is used as a means of control
3. Accomplishment:	Two-sided conversation Compromise
4. Feelings of Dad:	Concerned, worried, warm
Daughter:	Embarrassed, involved in decision
5. Long term Consequences:	Self-worth depends upon approval of others Comply out of guilt or anxiety

Figure 3. Parent-Adolescent Communication Style C Discussion Sheet.*

*Adapted by Darrell J. Burnett, Ph.D., with permission from Brownstone, J.E., and Dye, C.J. (1973). *Communication Workshop for Parents of Adolescents: Leader's Guide.* Champaign, IL: Research Press.

**Permission is granted to reproduce sufficient number of this figure to supply each participant with a copy.

DIRECTIONS:

1. One copy of Figure 4 is for each family.
2. Work together as a family.
3. Compare responses in your family to those listed for Style D.

ITEMS	RELATION TO STYLE D
1. Name:	Problem-oriented
2. Strengths:	Mutual compromise Two-sided caring Teaching son to think
3. Accomplishment:	Problem-solving alternatives discussed Input from both sides Assertion of feelings
4. Feelings of Mom:	Calm, assertive, warm, confident
Son:	Willing to compromise, feels involved
5. Long term Consequences:	Independence, self-confidence Rational approach to problem solving

Figure 4. Parent-Adolescent Communication Style D Discussion Sheet.*

*Adapted by Darrell J. Burnett, Ph.D., with permission from Brownstone, J.E., and Dye, C.J. (1973). *Communication Workshop for Parents of adolescents: Leader's Guide*. Champaign, IL: Research Press.

**Permission is granted to reproduce sufficient number of this figure to supply each participant with a copy.

Emphasize that, sometimes, due to an adolescent's immaturity or antisocial behavior, parents find themselves falling back to Styles "A," "B," or "C." Emphasize that an important aspect is being aware of various styles so that families do not become "locked in" to Style "A," "B," or "C."

26. Conclude by encouraging families to practice the problem-oriented Style "D," allowing all family members to recognize specific problems and to offer viable solutions.

27. As an introduction to Session 5, mention that, even if families agree to a problem-oriented style of communication, they have to realize that, within families, there are *three* basic personality types when it comes to solving problems. Mention that Session 5 will deal with the three basic **problem-solving approaches** in families.

PARENT-ADOLESCENT COMMUNICATION STYLES
Scripts*

Style A

Mom: Steve, will you come in here?

Son: Yes, Mom.

Mom: I should have said you *will* come in here! Do you know what I want to talk to you about?

Son: What?

Mom: You tell me!

Son: I'm late.

Mom: Do you know what time it is?

Son: Yes, Mother, I can read the clock.

Mom: Don't get smart with me young man! Why weren't you here hours ago?

Son: Do you want to know? Do you want to *listen* while I tell you?

Mom: Yes, I'll listen. I want to know why you weren't here.

Son: Well, we stopped for pizza after the game. They were real busy. It took us about an hour to get served. I couldn't get away. We were late.

Mom: There you go with those same old excuses! You remember not two weeks ago your father and I sat down and told you to be home at 10:30 every night!

Son: Here we go again.

Mom: You just keep that up, young man, you just keep that up!

Son: Now look, Mom, I'm not a kid anymore!

Mom: You're living in *my* house. You'll do what I want you to do! Now you're probably going to give me the silent treatment. You're probably going to go pout and shut up and not say anything.

Son: Whatever!

Mom: I want you to listen to me. When your father and I tell you to do something it's like you never hear a word we say! I'll bet right now you're not hearing a single word I say!

---

*Adapted by Darrell J. Burnett, Ph.D., with permission from Brownstone, J.E., and Dye, C.J. (1973). *Communication Workshop for Parents of Adolescents: Leader's Guide.* Champaign, IL: Research Press.

Son: I hear every word you say, Mother, every time you say it!

Mom: You just keep it up, young man, you just keep it up!

Son: Aw Mom.

Mom: Look, you can either follow the rules in our house, or you can leave!

Son: I will leave, just as soon as I'm old enough to get out of here.

Mom: You can leave right now! I'll help you pack!

Son: I wish I *could* leave!

Mom: Well I guess that means you're going to stay. That means you'll do what I tell you to do. And, to help you *learn* to do that, you're not going out for two weeks.

Son: Oh c'mon I wasn't doing anything bad; we couldn't get home any earlier.

Mom: You just keep that up and it'll be three weeks.

Son: Aw c'mon!

Mom: Alright, it's three weeks! And while you're staying in these three weeks maybe you'll think about being obedient to the rules your father and I set up.

Mom: Steve, I've been calling you and I'm not going to call you again.

Son: I just got a new tape and I wanted to listen to it on the big stereo in the family room.

Mom: Steve! Please come in here!

Son: OK, what do you want?

Mom: What do I want? You stand there with that look on your face and ask what do I want? What do you mean, what do I want?

Son: I don't know what you *want.* I've just been in the other room listening to a tape, and I have no way of knowing what you want!

Mom: Look around you. Look at your room. What's going on. What do you mean by this?

Son: What's wrong? Everything looks OK to me.

Mom: I can't believe it. I just don't know what I'm going to do with you. Now look, I bent over backwards for you. I told you if you didn't get this room cleaned up that you weren't going to that dance last Friday night at school. Then I gave in to you when you promised you'd clean it up the next day. You went to the dance, and you haven't even touched your room since then.

Son: Aw, Mom, hassle, hassle, hassle! That's all you do. You hassle me all the time! Besides the room's not that bad. And it's my room!

Mom: Well I just don't know what I'm going to do with you. Will you clean this up now, and I mean *now!* Or you're not going out the rest of the week. And I mean it!

Son: OK, OK, I'll do it in a minute.

Mom: Now, Steve. I want you to do it now!

Son: Mom, it's so silly to make such a big fuss over the room. I want to finish listening to my new tape now, just let me finish it, and then I'll do it. I promise.

Mom: Oh, just forget it. I'll do it myself. Just get out of here, and I'll do it myself.

Son: OK. Fine by me.

Dad: Linda, will you come in here a minute before you go upstairs?

Daughter: Sure Dad.

Dad: I'd like to talk with you right now.

Daughter: What about?

Dad: Do you know what time it is, Linda?

Daughter: I don't know, about 10:30 or 11?

Dad: Check your watch again. It must be stopped!

Daughter: Gee, I didn't know it was *that* late. I see what you mean. I guess it's pretty late.

Dad: Honey, do you realize how much we worry about you when you don't get in on time?

Daughter: I know you worry. But I was kind of in a bind tonight.

Dad: We worry an awful lot, you know!

Daughter: I would think you would trust me a little bit more than that, but I appreciate your worry.

Dad: Linda, it's not that we don't trust you. Sure we trust you. But we don't trust everybody else. Remember when we showed you that newspaper clipping about that young girl and what happened to her when she was out late? We don't want that to happen to you.

Daughter: I just didn't want to be the first to leave the group tonight. All the kids would have given me a hard time for going home so early and their parents don't seem to worry so much.

Dad: Maybe other parents don't worry so much about their kids. But then maybe other parents don't care so much about their kids.

Daughter: Yeah, I guess that's right.

Dad: And another thing. Did you notice how the lights all went on down the block when you slammed the car door and said good night to whomever that was in the car? What do you think the neighbors are going to think about parents who don't get their daughter in at a decent hour? What are they going to think about you? What are they going to think about us?

Daughter: Well, do you think maybe I could call you if it looked like I was going to be a little late?

Dad: Yeah, maybe about 15 minutes or so. But we couldn't take much longer wondering if anything was happening to you and what you were doing. We just want you to start coming in a little earlier, because we hate not knowing where you are or what's going on. Right now, I'd like you to go upstairs and write down all the reasons why we get so worried and concerned when you're late. Could you do that for us, now Sweetheart? And then we'll talk about it tomorrow.

Daughter: OK, Dad.

Mom: Steve?

Son: What?

Mom: Do you have a few minutes to talk?

Son: I'm going to listen to my new tape right now.

Mom: Well, when would you be free for us to talk?

Son: OK, what do you want?

Mom: We seem to have a real problem settling things about your room.

Son: You know, you bug me about this all the time.

Mom: Yeah, I know. It's really gotten to be a sore issue for both of us, hasn't it!

Son: Yeah, I don't know why you don't just leave me alone. I mean it's my room!

Mom: It seems like a big part of the problem is the way we've been talking to each other. I guess you feel it's your room, and I should just butt out!

Son: Well, I haven't been hassling you about it!

Mom: Well I feel hassled too, especially when I find myself rooting around your room to get your dirty clothes for washing. I was hoping you might have some suggestions so we could get together and end the hassling.

Son: Why can't we just agree that it's my room, and that there's no reason for anybody to go in there or look at it.

Mom: You'd like your room to be 100% off limits to everyone but you? Can you think what would happen if no one but you ever went into your room?

Son: I think that would be just fine with me!

Mom: Well, you know I've been taking responsibility for picking up your clothes, washing them, and putting them back away.

Son: Well, I guess I could get a hamper in my room and maybe put my dirty clothes in there.

Mom: Gee, sounds good so far! But how would the clothes get to the washing area and back to the room after they're washed?

Son: Well you've always taken care of that!

Mom: Right, and that's where the hassle began, with me in your room. You were mad because I was in there, and I was upset because when I was in there I felt like a maid. I've decided not to do that anymore.

Son: Well, I don't know. Let's see. Maybe I could take the clothes downstairs and then bring them up after they're washed. Especially, if that would mean that you would keep out of my room.

Mom: Great! Now let me make sure we both understand our agreement. I will stay out of the room, and I'll wash only the clothes you bring downstairs. You'll have more privacy, and you'll also take responsibility for taking your clothes downstairs and carrying them back to your room after they're washed. Is that right?

Son: Yeah, that's it.

PASSIVE, AGGRESSIVE, AND ASSERTIVE PROBLEM-SOLVING APPROACHES

GOALS

1. To help parents and adolescents identify and develop an assertive communication style within the family setting.

2. To help parents and adolescents distinguish among passive, aggressive, and assertive interactions within the family setting.

INFORMATION

Session 5 deals with passive, aggressive, and assertive problem-solving approaches. During this session, parents and adolescents discuss the fact that, within families, different family members use either a passive, aggressive, or assertive approach to solving family problems, based upon habit or personality or whatever feels "comfortable" for each family member.

Emphasize that an important point is for each member to be **aware** of his or her own way of responding. Encourage each member to attempt to increase assertive responses.

PROCEDURES

1. Direct family members—parents and adolescents—to sit together as families.

2. Tell them to turn to Form 8, "Three Problem-Solving Styles," in their *Participant Workbook* and as a family work together to complete the Form.

3. Poll the group members for their responses. Ask each family as a unit to give a definition of the term "passive." Record answers on the chalkboard.

4. Briefly, point out that the "passive" person tends to solve problems by "suffering" through them. (Passive comes from a Latin word meaning "to *suffer.*") Emphasize that the passive person usually communicates the following attitude: "Well, I don't like it, but I guess there's nothing I can do about it, so go ahead and do whatever you're going to do." Emphasize that the passive person often **whines** and **complains** while "giving in" and going along with whatever decision is made, but making sure that everyone knows that he or she doesn't like it. Emphasize that the passive person usually gets "walked on" by others.

5. Poll the group members for their definitions of "aggressive." Record the answers on the chalkboard.

6. Briefly point out that the aggressive person, in contrast to the passive person, approaches problems by taking over and, usually, "walking over" others involved. Emphasize that the aggressive person tries to solve problems by **humiliating, putting down,** and **becoming hostile towards** anyone else involved in the situation. Emphasize that the aggressive person often uses yelling as a way of gaining control in the family. Emphasize that the aggressive person usually makes accusatory "you" statements ("You don't know anything!", "You make me sick!", etc.).

7. Poll the group members for their definitions of "assertive." Record the answers on the chalkboard.

8. Briefly point out that the **assertive** person tries to solve problems by standing up for himself or herself, but respecting the rights of others. Emphasize that the assertive person attempts to use **logical, rational** approaches to problems and is often in search of a **meaningful compromise** within the family. Emphasize that assertive people "do not walk on others, nor do they allow others to walk on them." Emphasize that the assertive person, in contrast to the aggressive person, makes "I" statements (I think, I feel, etc.) rather than accusatory "you" statements. Emphasize that assertive problem solving is the goal for healthy family communications.

9. Following the brief discussion, distribute Figure 5, "How Assertive Behavior Differs from Passive and Aggressive Behavior." A copy is in the *Leader Manual.* (Permission is granted to reproduce sufficient number of this figure to supply each participant with a copy.) Make sure that each participant in the group has a copy. Briefly review the items on the handout. This serves as a summary of what has been discussed thus far. (Note: Do not start to work with Figure 5 until *after* you have discussed the definitions of passive, aggressive, and assertive. This encourages the participants to be involved in the discussion rather than simply looking at the sheets.)

10. Direct the parents and adolescents to Forms 9 and 10, "Problem-Solving Scripts," which are included in their *Participant Workbooks.*

11. Instruct the **parents** to fill out the scripts on Form 9, "Parent Response Sheet" and the **adolescents** to fill out the scripts on Form 10, "Adolescent Response Sheet."

12. Give the following instructions. "On the Response Sheet you have five family scenarios. Adolescents have five quotes from parents. Parents have five quotes from adolescents. You are expected to write typical 'quotes' which a **passive, aggressive,** or **assertive** person might make in response to each scene. For example, on the **adolescent** response

(Continued on page 41)

PASSIVE BEHAVIOR	ASSERTIVE BEHAVIOR	AGGRESSIVE BEHAVIOR
Whines or complains while "giving in."	Stands up for self but respects the rights of others	"Walks over" others with no respect for their rights.
Lets others choose for him/her	Chooses for self.	Chooses for others.
Inhibited expression of feelings	Rational, logical expression of feelings. ("I" statements).	Explosive, unpredictable expression of feelings. ("You" statements).
Feels hurt and anxious. Plays the "martyr" role.	Feels self confident. Feels good about self.	Feels defensive and hostile.
Does not achieve desired goals.	Achieves goals without harming others.	Achieves goals while harming others.

Figure 5. How assertive behavior differs from passive and aggressive behavior.*

*From *Your Perfect Right: A Guide to Assertive Living* (Sixth Edition) © 1990 by Robert E. Alberti and Michael L. Emmons. Adapted by Darrell J. Burnett, Ph.D., with permission of Impact Publishers, Inc., P.O. Box 1094, San Luis Obispo, CA 93406.

sheet the first scene is a quote from a parent saying 'I don't want you to hang around those kids anymore!'. Each adolescent is expected to write *three* different remarks as made by a passive, aggressive, and assertive adolescent in response to the parent statement. It doesn't matter if you personally are passive, aggressive, or assertive. This is just an activity to show that you know the differences and can write examples of each type of response. When you finish the first scene, go to the next quote from the parents and do the same thing until you have completed *all five scenes.* **Parents** are expected to do the same thing on the *parent* response sheet. For example, on the first scene is a quote from an adolescent saying, 'I'll hang around whatever kids I want to!'. Each parent, mom and dad separately, is expected to write *three* different remarks representing a ***passive, aggressive,*** or ***assertive*** parent. Do all *five* scenes."

13. Allow 15 to 20 minutes for the completion of the 15 responses. Walk around the room while the participants are writing their quotes, offering suggestions as needed. Emphasize that the ***passive*** person does not simply give in, but gives in while ***complaining*** and ***whining.*** (Some group members may tend to present the passive person simply as giving in and saying "okay" without including the whining and complaining.)

14. Ask for samples after all responses have been written for all five scenes, first from adolescents, then from parents.

15. Ask the adolescents to read aloud their "passive" responses to the first scene.

16. Ask the parents to read aloud their "passive" responses to the first scene.

17. Ask the adolescents to read aloud their "aggressive" responses to the first scene.

18. Ask the parents to read aloud their "aggressive" responses to the first scene.

19. Ask the adolescents to read aloud their "assertive" responses to the first scene.

20. Ask the parents to read aloud their "assertive" responses to the first scene.

21. Direct the members of each family unit—parents and adolescents—to review their responses with each other on the other four scenes.

22. After five minutes emphasize that an important point is to become **aware** of the various personalities in the family, and how each chooses passive, aggressive, or assertive approaches.

23. Remind the families that the **assertive** approach is the goal for healthy family communications, wherein each member is able to stand up for himself or herself, and to "get his or her point across" in family discussions.

24. Conclude by introducing the next few sessions as practice sessions in **assertive communications** wherein parents and adolescents will practice the **techniques of effective communication** which will allow each family member to practice getting his or her point across effectively with other family members.

FEELINGS CONCERNING FAMILY ISSUES

GOALS

1. To help parents and adolescents identify and develop assertive communications within the family setting.

2. To help parents and adolescents learn effective communication techniques including (a) nonverbal techniques, (b) staying on topic, and (c) listening while discussing topics connected with family living.

INFORMATION

The sixth session is a hands-on exercise in effective communication, teaching parents and adolescents how to get their ideas and feelings across in the most effective way possible.

Emphasize the following points:

- In many families, various members are not actively involved in solving family problems because they lack skills in

    1. **WHAT** they say,
    2. **HOW** they say it, or in
    3. **LISTENING** to what others say.

- The next few sessions will offer them specific practice in these three skills.

PROCEDURES

1. Direct adolescents and parents to sit together.

2. Briefly explain that **effective communication** is essential in learning assertive family problem solving.

3. Direct participants to Form 11, "Major Areas of Effective Communication" (copy is in the *Participant Workbook*). Make sure that each participant has a copy.

4. Review the three basic elements of effective communication as outlined on Form 11. Explain each element as follows.

5. Emphasize that **what** you say is important in family problem solving because often, in families, the members get "off the track" and tend to be vague and unclear.

   Encourage parents and adolescents to **stay on topic** and to be **specific** as they communicate with each other.

   Emphasize that, often, when discussing a specific issue, such as curfew, parents ramble onto topics of grades, friends, clothes, etc., rather than staying on the topic of curfew.

   Emphasize that often parents' expectations are vaguely expressed to the adolescent, such as "good grades," "respect," or "nice friends." Emphasize that adolescents often speak of wanting more "freedom" without getting specific as to what "freedom" entails for them.

6. Emphasize that perhaps the biggest roadblock to effective family communications is **how** you say what you have to say. Emphasize that often family members have very good ideas and solutions to family problems, but the **way** they present their ideas "turns off" the other family members.

7. Give the following examples of each of the nonverbal techniques listed on Form 11: eye contact, tone of voice, and posture.

EYE CONTACT: Give a compliment to an adolescent participant in the group (Example: "I really like that shirt you're wearing!"), saying the same thing three times. Say it once while **looking at the floor.** Say it again while **looking at the ceiling.** Say it a third time while **looking directly at the person** you are complimenting. Emphasize the importance of **looking** at the person to whom you're talking.

TONE OF VOICE: Give the same compliment to the same person in the group, but repeat it several times, giving examples of the tone of voice and how it affects communication. Say the words "Nice shirt." Say the words once in a **mumbling,** almost **inaudible** tone. Say the words again in a **loud** and **boisterous** tone. Then, say "Nice shirt. It used to be in style 10 years ago!" Explain how this **sarcastic** tone offends people.

POSTURE: Demonstrate body posture as described in Form 11 (Example, **yawn** while saying "nice shirt" to the same participant). Emphasize the importance of appearing sincere and interested when communicating by **leaning towards** someone when you are speaking to them. Give one final example with the same participant while leaning towards the participant while saying "Nice shirt!"

(Thank the participant for allowing you to use his or her shirt as an example, and tell the participant you really do like the shirt!)

8. Ask a group member how he or she knows someone is **listening** to him or her. Emphasize that the most certain way to know if someone is listening to you is if he or she can **repeat** what you just said.

Emphasize that often, in families, we **presume** that the other person is listening to what we say. Emphasize the importance of **checking out** whether family members are listening to what we are saying.

Emphasize how good listening promotes good speaking and vice versa.

9. After explaining the basics on Form 11, "Major Areas of Effective Communication," explain that they are now going to **practice** these basics with each other as individual families using a **scoring grid** and some **family topics** while grading each other in a family communication activity.

10. Direct their attention to Form 12, "Scoring Grid for Effective Communication on Family Topics," which gives the **directions** for the communication activity. (Copy is in *Participant Workbook.*)

11. Direct their attention also to Form 13, "Family Topics for an Effective Communication Activity." (Copy is in the *Participant Workbook.*) **NOTE:** Each family needs only one scoring grid (Form 12) and one *"family topics"* list (Form 13). However, extra copies should be available as needed.

12. Explain that with the use of the *scoring grid* and the sheet of *family topics* each family will have the opportunity to practice the *three* areas of communication: using **nonverbal communication techniques, staying on topic,** and **listening.**

13. Emphasize that the activity can be done with either three members (two parents and an adolescent) or *two* members (a parent and an adolescent). In the case of three members, one parent interacts with the adolescent while the *other parent scores* the parent and adolescent on the scoring grid. In the case of only two family members, parent and adolescent *score each other.*

14. Demonstrate the activity as follows.

    a. Instruct the families to fill in the first line of the scoring grid with two names, placing the *adolescent's* name under the *speaker* column, and *parent's* name under the *listener* column on the same line (see Figure 6, "Example of a Partially Completed Scoring Grid" in the *Leader Manual*).

b.   Call the participants' attention to the steps outlined on the directions section on Form 12 (Scoring Grid).

c.   Explain that step *one* requires the speaker to talk on the topic listed on the Family Topics sheet, with at least *two sentences* per response. For example, the first topic is "If I could change my family to make it better, I would . . ." The speaker is expected to complete this sentence with at least two sentences. Explain that, while giving the response, the *speaker* is to address the *listener*, paying attention to the nonverbal techniques of eye contact, tone of voice, and posture, as listed on the scoring grid. The speaker is also to be mindful of being specific, staying on topic, and not rambling. This is scored under the heading of *"content"* on the scoring grid.

d.   Explain that step *two* requires the *listener* to repeat back what the *speaker* has just said with **no added commentary.** Thus, in the example above, the listener would repeat "You just said that if you could change your family to make it better, you would . . . etc., etc., etc." Emphasize that the listener's task is simply to **repeat accurately** what the speaker says to **prove** to the speaker that he or she is listening.

e.   Explain that step *three* involves **scoring** the speaker and listener on the criteria listed on the scoring grid: **eye contact** (the extent to which the speaker is looking at the listener, or the extent to which the listener is looking at the speaker when repeating back what was said); **tone of voice** (the extent to which the speaker and listener use appropriate tones in contrast to a threatening, sarcastic, lecturing, whining, too loud or too soft tone of voice); **posture** (the extent to which the body language of the speaker and listener

(Continued on Page 49)

List Name of Speaker	Areas to Score				List Name of Listener	Areas to Score			
	Eye Contact	Tone of Voice	Posture	Content		Eye Contact	Tone of Voice	Posture	Content
JOHN	1	2	2	3	Mom	2	3	2	2
Mom	2	2	3	2	JOHN	2	1	2	2
JOHN	2	3	2	1	DAD	2	1	3	2
DAD	2	3	3	3	JOHN	3	2	3	2

Score: 1 = Good (has the general idea, but needs lots of practice)
2 = Very Good (doing well, but still needs some practice)
3 = Excellent (no problems)

Figure 6. Examples of a partially completed scoring grid for the effective communication activity.

convey interest and concern (leaning toward the person) rather than boredom (yawing, slouching, hand supporting chin, etc.), defensiveness (arms folded tightly against body), or aggressiveness (finger-pointing). As noted above, *"content"* refers to the **contents** of what is said and measures how well the **speaker stays on topic,** avoids rambling, is specific and clear. It also measures how well the **listener** is able to **repeat** what the speaker says without becoming **defensive** or without **adding** material or wandering into other topics.

f. Call participants' attention to the bottom of the scoring grid, which lists the grading numbers:

> 1 = **good** (has the general idea, but needs lots of practice)
>
> 2 = **very good** (doing well, but still needs practice)
>
> 3 = **excellent** (no problem!)

Emphasize that everyone gets at least a *"good,"* and there are **no** "0" scores.

g. Explain the scoring procedure as follows:

When there are **two parents** and an adolescent, **one parent scores,** observing how the **speaker** communicates with the listener, and how the listener repeats back what the speaker says. The scorer then grades the speaker on **each** of the **four** items on the scoring grid (eye contact, tone of voice, posture, and content), placing a number (1,2,or 3) under each item. The scorer does the same for the **listener.**

When only **one parent** and one adolescent are present, they score each other **after each completed interaction** (that is, after the speaker has communicated to the listener, and the listener has repeated what was said). Thus, the **listener scores the speaker** and the **speaker scores the listener.**

Explain that when the numbers are given, the scorer should explain *why* the particular numbers were chosen. Thus, a scorer might say "I gave you a "1" on eye contact because although you started out looking at the other person, you began to drift with your eyes and then avoided eye contact most of the time."

h. Explain that, after the scoring has taken place for the speaker and listener, they change roles, with the **listener** becoming the **speaker,** and the **speaker** becoming the **listener** on the **same topic.** Thus, in the example above, the parent who was the listener becomes the speaker, with the parent's name listed under the speaker column. The adolescent becomes the listener, with the adolescent's name listed under the listener column. The same topic is repeated, "If I could change my family to make it better, I would . . ."

Explain that **each** family member addresses each topic on the sheet.

Explain that, in the case of **two parents** and an adolescent, the **parents take turns scoring,** so that **both** parents get involved in interacting with the adolescent. **NOTE:** The exercise calls for **one parent** to score the interaction between the adolescent and the other parent.

15. Instruct the families to begin the activity, starting with the item on the top of the Family Topics sheet (Form 13), and continue through each item. Remind them again that **each** family member should address **each** item.

16. Move from family to family while they practice, giving guidance where necessary. Make sure that they don't get "bogged down" on any specific topic. Help them concentrate on the nonverbal techniques. Help the listener to simply repeat what is said without adding more material or becoming defensive.

17. Allow 25 to 30 minutes for the activity. Have extra scoring grids to use if needed.

18. Ask if anyone had any difficulty with listening without becoming **defensive,** or any difficulty being **specific.**

19. Explain that unqualified **listening** is the first part of communicating when a problem exists. Explain that, after you have proven to a family member that you have heard his or her point of view, then you can offer yours. Explain that these activities are aimed at simply practicing how to get your point across, and how to listen objectively.

20. Emphasize the importance of being **specific** when communicating.

21. Conclude by noting that the scoring grid simply allows family members to stay on focus while discussing issues. Emphasize that the scoring grid will be used in the next three sessions as the topics become more **personal** and the family members begin to practice making **"I" statements** toward each other.

22. Introduce the next session by noting that the scoring grid will be used while the family members practice how to express **positive** feelings toward each other, practicing how to **give** and **receive compliments.**

EXPRESSING POSITIVE FEELINGS TOWARD FAMILY MEMBERS

GOALS

1. To help parents and adolescents identify and develop assertive communications within the family setting.

2. To help parents and adolescents learn effective communication techniques including (a) nonverbal techniques, (b) staying on topic, and (c) listening while expressing *positive* feelings toward each other.

INFORMATION

Session 7 is a hands-on activity in effective communication, teaching parents and adolescents nonverbal techniques while exchanging "I" statements of *positive* feelings toward each other.

Emphasize the following points:

- Positive interactions in families with adolescents are very important in order to counter the almost inevitable negative interactions which take place as the adolescent struggles toward his or her independence.

- Children, in the early stages of life, develop patterns for **gaining attention** within the family. Emphasize that a child has a choice of gaining attention through **positive** behaviors or through **negative** behaviors. Explain that, in many families, the tendency is to give attention **only** when **negative** behaviors occur. Thus, parents are not accustomed to saying "Johnny, what a good boy, you didn't break your sister's toy today!". Rather, Johnny usually receives **no** attention in that case. Usually the attention comes when he **does break** a toy.

- In many cases, the child develops a repertoire of **negative** behaviors because he or she can get **attention** for them. Emphasize that, in some cases, some children see being good as "boring."

- Breaking the chain of "negative attention" and attending to positive behaviors is very important. Emphasize that in the average healthy family, the ratio of **positive** to **negative** interactions should be **four to one.** Thus, for each incident where attention is given for **negative** behaviors, **four** incidents should occur where attention is given for **positive** behaviors.

- Activities for this session, with the emphasis upon positives, are a step toward increasing positive interactions in families.

PROCEDURES

1. Direct parents and adolescents to sit together.

2. Introduce the session by making the points listed above about positive and negative attention in families.

3. Direct participants to Form 14, "Scoring Grid for Effective Communication of Positive Feelings," and Form 15, "Stem Statements of Positive Feelings for an Effective Communication Activity." (Copy of each is in the *Participant Workbook.*)

4. Briefly review the items on Form 11, "Major Areas of Effective Communication," noting the importance of staying on topic, using nonverbal techniques, and listening, as explained during Session 6.

5. Briefly review the directions for using the scoring grid, as explained during Session 6.

6. Instruct the families to complete Form 14, "Scoring Grid for Effective Communication of Positive Feelings," as they did in Session 6, but this time using Form 15, "Stem Statements of Positive Feelings for an Effective Communication Activity," with "I" statements.

7. Emphasize that, on the scoring grid, under the item **"content,"** the important point is to stay on topic, and stay **positive** with **no negative qualifiers.** Explain that, at times, compliments are given within families, only to be **undone** by a negative statement. Give an example of how a negative statement undoes a compliment, as when a parent says "Nice job on the English, you got a 'C';" but then follows with a statement such as "It's about time, after getting a 'D' and an 'F'!"

   Emphasize also that the **listener,** when repeating the positive statement by the speaker, simply repeats the positive, **without minimizing** the compliment with a **negative qualifier.** Using the example above, if the parent says "Nice job in English, you got a 'C';" the adolescent should simply repeat the statement, and not qualify it. Thus, the important point is for the adolescent to accept the compliment and **not** say "The English teacher is an easy grader. He never gives lower than a 'C' to anybody."

8. Remind participants to start with the first sentence at the top of the sheet, and to do **each** item on the sheet, with each family member addressing **each** item on the sheet.

9. If any new families are in the group, instruct them individually on how to complete the activity. Move around the room reminding the participants to remain positive, with no negative qualifiers.

10. Allow 25 to 30 minutes for families to do the activity.

11. Ask participants whether or not they had problems staying positive and/or finding enough positive statements to make. Ask whether eye contact was a problem. Ask whether people were embarrassed while giving or receiving compliments.

12. Conclude by reiterating the importance of positive interactions. Remind parents and adolescents to continue to **look for positive** things in each other and to make "I" statements about positive feelings towards each other.

13. Introduce the next session by noting that, although the emphasis has been on positive feelings, the reality is that **negative** feelings also exist toward family members, and an avenue is needed within families for each member to express negative feelings. Emphasize that the freedom to make negative statements gives **more meaning** to positive statements. Emphasize that the next session will center around **constructive, appropriately stated** negative feelings, with no yelling, screaming, or put-down remarks. Emphasize that the session will encourage **assertive,** not **aggressive** communication.

EXPRESSING NEGATIVE FEELINGS TOWARD FAMILY MEMBERS

GOALS

1. To help parents and adolescents identify and develop assertive communication within the family setting.

2. To help parents and adolescents learn effective communication techniques including (a) nonverbal techniques, (b) staying on topic and (c) listening while expressing **negative** feelings toward each other.

INFORMATION

Session 8 is a hands-on activity in effective communication, allowing parents and adolescents to practice nonverbal techniques while exchanging "I" statements of negative feelings toward each other.

Emphasize the following points:

- Negative statements between family members sometimes lead to emotional outbursts, temper tantrums, property destruction, and a general feeling of unrest.

- Negative feelings are a **continuum,** often beginning as feelings of being **annoyed.** These feelings can then develop into feelings of **resentment,** which, in turn, can develop into **anger** and ultimately **hatred.**

- An important point is for families to be able to discuss feelings of **annoyance** and **resentment as they occur,** so that they don't build into strong feelings of anger and hatred over a period of years. Emphasize that, in families these strong feelings of **anger** and **hatred** are what lead to the explosive outbursts within the family settings.

- Within healthy family settings the need exists to have **freedom** to express **disagreement** and negative feelings which are accepted as constructive criticism.

- Adolescents often have a difficult time expressing negative feelings without becoming either **aggressive** or **passive** and withdrawn.

- Exchanging negative feelings appropriately is a major but essential task for effective communication in a family. Note that, unless family members feel the **freedom** to make negative statements within the family, the positive statements do not have the same value. That is, unless a person feels free to say "no" within the family, the "yes" statement often may be out of fear.

- During this activity each family member will have an opportunity to begin to develop an atmosphere in the family where **appropriate** expression of negative feelings is acceptable.

PROCEDURES

1. Direct parents and adolescents to sit together.

2. Introduce the session by discussing the points listed above about (a) the importance of allowing the expression of

negative feelings between and among family members; and (b) the continuum of feelings as follows:

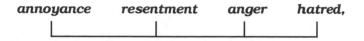

annoyance   resentment   anger   hatred,

and the need to practice how to express negative feelings assertively.

Draw the continuum on the chalkboard, and explain that this activity centers around the first two parts of the continuum, **"annoyance"** and **"resentment."** Explain that if feelings of annoyance and resentment are expressed early, they often will not build to anger and hatred.

3. Direct participants to Form 16, "Scoring Grid for Effective Communication of Negative Feelings," and Form 17, "Stem Statements of Negative Feelings for an Effective Communication Activity." (Both Forms are in the *Participant Workbook*.) Have extra scoring grid sheets available for use if needed.

4. Briefly review the items on Form 11, "Major Areas of Effective Communication," noting the importance of **staying on topic,** using **nonverbal** techniques, and **listening,** as originally explained in Session 6.

5. Briefly review the directions for using the scoring grid, as explained during Session 6.

6. Explain that the families will complete Form 16, "Scoring Grid for Effective Communication of Negative Feelings," similarly to the way they did Forms 12 and 14 in Sessions 6 and 7, but this time using Form 17, "Stem Statements of Negative Feelings" with "I" statements.

7. Emphasize that, on the scoring grid, under the item **"tone of voice,"** the important point is to maintain an assertive, not aggressive tone, using a **calm** voice, with **no yelling, threatening, or offensive language.** Emphasize that the activity is one in learning to be appropriate while

disagreeing. It is **not** a screaming match or an exercise in **put-downs.**

8. Emphasize that the **"content"** item on the scoring grid refers to **what** is **actually said** by the speaker and listener. Emphasize that the exercise is a beginning in learning how to **negotiate.** That is, when two people disagree with each other, and attempt to negotiate a compromise, it is initially important for each person to make his or her point **assertively** without the other person becoming **defensive.** Emphasize that this activity involves a speaker and a listener. The **speaker** is expected to communicate clearly, specifically, and **assertively** while making his or her point about a specific area in which the speaker is having difficulty with the listener. The **listener** is expected to show that he or she is listening by **simply repeating** the statement made by the speaker without becoming **defensive.** Thus, on the scoring grid, under the column marked "content," the **speaker** is graded on being **assertive,** not aggressive. That is, the speaker is expected to simply make his or her "I" statement about his or her opinion or feelings about the other person. The **listener** is graded on the scoring grid under the column "content" in terms of whether the listener simply repeats the statement made by the speaker **without attempting to defend** himself or herself or to challenge the speaker, even though the listener may disagree with what the speaker is saying.

Emphasize that no one likes to hear negative things about himself or herself, and that the normal tendency, if you disagree with what you hear, is to challenge the statement immediately. However, in this phase of communication training the simple, **objective repetition** of the statement is simply to prove to the speaker that the listener is indeed listening.

Emphasize that, in the normal sequence of negotiations, the **next step** would be for the listener to make a **self-defense statement,** covering the areas of disagreement. However, in this activity the **first** step is the **only** one practiced, namely, **simply repeating** what is said.

Give the following example:

>If the adolescent, as speaker, addresses dad and says, "I feel irritated when you put me down in front of my friends," the tendency for dad, the listener, who disagrees with what the adolescent said, might be to repeat the statement, but with his own self-defense added. Thus, dad might be tempted to say, "You just said that you feel irritated when I put you down in front of your friends, **BUT** there's no way I do that very often. I think I may have done it once, and I think **you're** overreacting!"

>Emphasize that the activity calls for dad simply to **repeat** the statement and leave out his self-defensive response (beginning with BUT . . .).

9. Remind participants to start with the **first** sentence at the top of Form 17, "Stem Statements of Negative Feelings" and to do **each** sentence, with each family member addressing each sentence on the sheet.

10. If any new families are in the group, instruct them individually on how to complete the activity. Move around the room reminding participants to remain **assertive** and **not aggressive.**

11. Allow 25 to 30 minutes for families to do the activity. Remind all families to remain calm, stay on topic, and not to get "stuck" on any one sentence for a long time. Remind them that this is simply an activity in learning to give and receive negative feelings without turning the interaction into a major negative outburst.

12. After the allotted time, ask participants to discuss the ease or difficulty of the task.

13. Ask them to compare this session with the previous session which emphasized positives rather than negatives. Ask them which session was easier and why. (**NOTE:** Some may report "positives" were easier because they had no **fear of retaliation.** Others may report that "negatives" were easier because they had more **"material"** to discuss.)

14. Compliment participants for their participation during this session and the last session, noting that they have had an opportunity to communicate on a level far more **intense** than typical parent-adolescent communications within the average family.

15. Conclude by encouraging participants to keep the "feelings" sheets for future use, to continue practicing communications, and to be aware of their everyday use of nonverbal communication techniques.

16. Introduce Session 9, on **empathy,** by noting that although being able to express and listen to feelings and opinions among family members is important, attempting to "put one's self in the other family member's shoes" concerning family members' feelings and opinions is equally important. Explain that parents and adolescents will practice empathy during the next session, attempting to see and feel things from each other's point of view.

EXPRESSING FEELINGS OF EMPATHY TOWARD FAMILY MEMBERS

GOALS

1. To help parents and adolescents identify and develop assertive communications with the family setting.

2. To help parents and adolescents develop **empathy** for each other, ***"getting into each other's shoes"*** concerning feelings, opinions, and thoughts connected with parent-adolescent issues.

3. To help parents and adolescents learn effective communication techniques including (a) nonverbal techniques, (b) staying on topic, and (c) listening while expressing feelings of empathy toward each other.

INFORMATION

Session 9 is a hands-on activity in effective communication, allowing parents and adolescents to practice (a) specific nonverbal techniques, (b) staying on topic, and (c) listening while expressing feelings of empathy toward each other.

Emphasize the following points:

- The importance of **empathy** should be stressed in the development of effective assertive communication. Emphasize that aggression is often an obstacle to assertive interactions. That is, family members run the risk of becoming aggressive, hostile, defensive, and belittling toward each other when a **sensitive** topic is discussed. Aggressive family members are often somewhat **insensitive** to the needs or feelings of each other.

- Empathy, the process of "getting into the other person's shoes," counteracts the tendency toward aggressive insensitivity.

- If a family member can become aware of another member's feelings and can try to get inside that member's feelings, thoughts, etc., then family members can more easily become assertive rather than aggressive.

- Empathy comes from the Greek word meaning "to suffer **inside.**" Sympathy means "to suffer **with.**" Empathy is much deeper than sympathy.

PROCEDURES

1. Direct parents and adolescents to sit apart from each other on opposite sides of the room.

2. Introduce the topic of empathy with the points listed in the "Information" section of this Session.

3. Call participants' attention to Forms 18 and 19 with activities on empathy related to family issues. (A copy of each form is found in *Participant Workbook*.) (**NOTE:** If this workshop is taking place in an inpatient psychiatric hospital, the leader may choose Forms 21 and 22 related to "Hospital Issues" which are discussed at the end of the material in this session.)

4. Direct the parents, mom and dad separately, to fill out Form 18, "*Parent* Sheet for Activities on Empathy Related to Family Issues." Have adolescents fill out Form 19 "*Adolescent* Sheet for Activities on Empathy Related to Family Issues." Direct adolescents to distinguish how mom and dad feel separately on each issue. Have extra sheets available for use if needed.

5. Explain that Part A of the Form addresses feelings of the **other family member** in connection with basic issues which usually arise in the course of adolescence. Explain that Part B of the Form addresses feelings of the **person completing the sheet.** Emphasize that *both* sections are to be completed. (**NOTE:** If they haven't experienced some of the issues yet, direct them to **anticipate** possible feelings, thoughts, etc.)

6. Remind parents and adolescents that the task is to try to "get into each other's shoes," **whether agreement exists or not.** (**NOTE:** If a parent or adolescent hesitates or says he or she doesn't **know** what the other family member feels or thinks, instruct each participant to **guess.**)

7. Allow 20 minutes for completion of the Forms.

8. Direct parents and adolescents to sit together as families while reviewing the **completed** sheets.

9. Explain that various items will be discussed among family members in a **structured** fashion, using Form 20, "Scoring Grid for Effective Communication of Empathy."

10. Give the following instructions.

    a. The **parent** begins the interaction as **speaker.** The adolescent is the listener. Their names are entered on the scoring grid.

    b. The parent speaks to the adolescent, attempting to **empathize,** to "get into the adolescent's shoes" on the first item listed on Form 18, Part A (i.e., the adolescent is at a party and friends encourage him or her to drink alcohol). The parent expresses what he or she thinks the adolescent might think or feel when facing peer pressure. The parent addresses the remarks *directly* to the adolescent.

c. The **adolescent,** as **listener,** simply **repeats** back what the parent says, to show that he or she was listening.

d. The speaker and listener are then **scored** on Form 20, the scoring grid (eye contact, etc.), either by a third scorer if two parents are present, or by themselves if only one parent is present.

e. The **adolescent** then becomes the **speaker** on the **same topic,** explaining to the **parent,** as **listener,** that, indeed the parent was correct about the adolescent's feelings or thoughts. If the parent omitted certain thoughts or feelings which the adolescent had, then the adolescent communicates them to the parent.

f. The **parent,** as **listener,** simply **repeats** back what is said.

g. Scoring on the scoring grid then takes place as above.

h. After this interaction, the **adolescent** becomes the **speaker,** attempting to **empathize** with the parent on the first item on Form 19, Part A (i.e., dealing with the first unchaperoned date), attempting to "get into the parent's shoes" concerning feelings and thoughts which might make it difficult for the parent to deal with the situation.

i. The **parent,** as **listener,** simply **repeats** what the adolescent said.

j. The two are scored on the scoring grid, Form 20.

k. The **parent** then becomes the **speaker** on the **same topic,** explaining that, indeed, the adolescent was correct about the parent's feelings or thoughts. If the adolescent omitted any feelings or thoughts which the parent had, or might have, the parent communicates this to the adolescent.

l.   The adolescent then simply **repeats** what the parent said.

m. The two are then scored on the scoring grid, Form 20.

11. Explain that this procedure is used for **each** of the items on the empathy sheets (Forms 18 and 19) until **all** items have been discussed, as time permits.

12. Emphasize the importance of remaining **calm** and **staying on task** during the activity.

13. Allow 20 minutes for completing the scoring grid.

14. Briefly ask group members to discuss whether they had difficulty remaining on topic and remaining calm.

15. Conclude by noting that empathy is an essential for good communications in families. Encourage continued practice in this area.

16. Introduce Session 10 by noting that empathy becomes easier the more we **understand** experiences and behaviors of family members. Accordingly, Part III of the program, Sessions 10 through 15, centers around understanding the "whys" and "wherefores" of behaviors which occur within families and among family members. Explain that the sessions will deal with the **principles of behavior change.**

Briefly note that Session 10 will deal with the topic of how **behaviors** and their **consequences** are intimately connected so that consequences can actually determine whether certain behaviors occur again.

NOTE: If Session 9 takes place in an inpatient psychiatric setting, the leader may opt to use the *"Hospital Issues"*

Empathy Sheets, Forms 21 and 22, using the same format as listed above, but substituting *"Hospital Issues"* for *"Family Issues."* In this case, the adolescents and parents attempt to empathize with each other in connection with the various **phases** of the hospitalization (pre-admission, admission, visits, passes, discharge, etc.). Since these issues and experiences are current and intense, the session needs much structure to keep the participants on task.

Part III

RECOGNIZING
BEHAVIOR
AS A
FUNCTION
OF ITS
CONSEQUENCE

THE LAW
OF EFFECT

GOALS

1. To help parents and adolescents understand why behaviors occur, and to learn some techniques for changing and/or managing behaviors within the home setting.

2. To help parents and adolescents understand the Law of Effect: the relationship between behavior and its consequence.

INFORMATION

Session 10 begins a series of sessions centering around why behaviors occur. This session and the next session involve more lecturing by the group leader than in previous settings, however the information is basic.

The main topic for Session 10 is the Law of Effect, which states that **behavior** is a **function** of its **consequence.** That is, the probability of a behavior recurring is based upon how a person **experiences** and **perceives** the consequences which come after the behavior. Thus, if a person experiences or perceives a consequence as **pleasant,** he or she is likely to **repeat** the behavior. However, if a person experiences or perceives a consequence as **unpleasant,** he or she is likely to decrease that behavior in the future.

Emphasize the following points:

- The key to the repetition or decrease of the behavior is based upon how the person **perceives** or **experiences** the **consequence** for the behavior. For example, some people get a traffic ticket, and they experience this as an extremely unpleasant and negative consequence. They then significantly decrease their erratic and problematic driving habits. However, some people need more than one ticket before they experience the consequence as unpleasant. Indeed, some people need threats from insurance companies concerning increased premiums before they will ultimately change their driving habits to concur with the rules of the road.

- With families, one child or adolescent may perceive a consequence as **unpleasant,** while another brother or sister may perceive the **same** consequence as **pleasant.**

- The **individual difference** in the **perception** and **experience** of **consequences** is what accounts for some children in the family **decreasing** their negative behaviors while other siblings **continue** them.

- Each adolescent finds his or her **limits** while acting out during adolescence, based upon what he or she experiences as the **ultimate** negative consequence which the adolescent wants to avoid in the future. A continuum of **negative** consequences can be applied to an adolescent, ranging from a simple **lecture** or warning, and proceeding all the way to **prison!**

- Fortunately, most adolescents stop short of needing the **legal** system as a consequence for stopping their behaviors. However, in some situations an adolescent will stop his or her antisocial activities only if forced to do so, legally. Thus, in some cases, in order to bring an adolescent under control, the necessary procedure is to **press charges.** Indeed, sometimes, "love means pressing charges."

PROCEDURES

1. Direct parents and adolescents to sit together.

2. Introduce the session by reading, or handing out the following scenario, asking the parents to put themselves in the place of the parents described in the scenario:

> A fifteen year old boy is living at home with his parents. Over the past six months, several problems have occurred. The boy has had four separate instances of **truancy.** He has been caught twice with **marijuana** at home. Eight instances of **curfew violation** have been identified. He has **run away** from home on two occasions, once for four days, and once for ten days. Two incidences of **stealing** have occurred, once from the family ($50), and once in the community (shoplifting $80 worth of tapes). No charges were pressed in either incident, and the parents made restitution to the store. During the past **six** months the parents have been involved with their son in **family counseling,** beginning with the school counselor, then the pastoral counselor, and recently in outpatient family therapy. On this particular day, as mother returns home at 4 PM she walks into the house and finds a letter from school that is torn, crumpled, and thrown on the sofa. She reads the letter and is informed that her son has been truant three times within the past two weeks. She also reads that he is about to flunk three of his courses. She walks toward his room. As she opens the door she finds him smoking marijuana. She confronts him with increased "grounding." He retaliates by cursing at her. He runs out of his room, pushes her aside, and runs out the front door. As he runs down the driveway he picks up a rock and throws it at the family car, denting it. He picks up another rock, and throws it at the front windshield, cracking it. He then runs down the street yelling obscenities, making obscene gestures toward his mother, and runs away.

3. After going over the scenario, ask each parent to mentally **choose one** (and only one) of the following reactions to this scenario:

a.   go after the boy to find him,

b.   get more strict with house rules,

c.   seek more family counseling, or

d.   press charges for the damage to the car.

4. **Before** the parents respond, ask the **adolescents** how they think their parents would respond. Ask each adolescent individually.

5. Poll the parents for their individual responses. Record them on the chalkboard. For those parents who did not choose "d. press charges," ask them **why** they did not choose to press charges. (They will usually express concern about issues such as making things worse, or getting involved with criminals and learning worse habits, or some may discuss frustration with the lack of legal action for "family" matters.)

     For those parents who **did** chose "pressing charges," ask them **why.** (They will usually describe this approach as the "last chance" when nothing else has worked.)

6. After the discussion by the parents about how they would have handled the scenario (allow up to 15 minutes), introduce the topic of how **consequences** following behaviors play an essential part in determining whether the behaviors will occur again. Emphasize how, in some cases, the **legal** consequence, drastic though it may seem, may be the only **real** consequence which will stop the problem behavior.

7. Introduce the topic of the LAW OF EFFECT, directing the participants to Form 23, "The Law of Effect: Behavior Is a Function of Its Consequence" (copy is in *Participant Workbook*). Discuss those points listed in the "Information" section about how behavior is a function of its consequence, noting the importance of the **perception** and **experience** of the consequence.

8. Emphasize that, as mentioned on Form 23, the task of parents with adolescents is to communicate to them that there are **unpleasant** consequences for **problem** behaviors at home, school, and in the community, and that there are **pleasant** consequences for **positive** behaviors.

9. Direct the participants to look at the bottom half of Form 23, "The Law of Effect," under the heading entitled *"The Continuum of Unpleasant Consequences"* as to what an adolescent may experience. Note that each adolescent eventually will "bottom out," stopping the problem behavior when the consequence is **perceived** and **experienced** as unpleasant enough to avoid in the future.

10. Explain that you will go through each setting (home, school, community, and probation) listed on Form 23, noting the continuum of negative consequences for problem behaviors in those settings. Note how some adolescents stop their problem behaviors earlier than others, based upon how they **perceive** and **experience** the consequences as they proceed along the continuum of more severe consequences.

11. Discuss the HOME setting and give an example of a problem behavior (i.e., curfew violation). Give examples of the continuum of consequences which parents can apply at home (first a lecture, then restriction, then counseling, then probation). Give examples of how some adolescents perceive and experience a **lecture** or **warning** from parents as significantly unpleasant enough to stop the behavior.

Note, however, that some adolescents are not affected by lectures or warnings and do not perceive or experience them as unpleasant. In fact, lectures and warnings may be "pleasant" for some adolescents because they enjoy seeing their parents get upset!

Discuss how **restriction,** or grounding, the next level on the continuum of negative consequences, stops some adolescents because it is indeed unpleasant to them. They never thought mom or dad would actually "carry through" with the warning of restriction. Note, however, that some adolescents are not affected by restriction because it actually becomes a "game." They reason, "If I'm on restriction, my parents are on restriction!". The adolescent also may see a restriction as simply a short "time out" while he or she regroups his or her energy to plan bigger and better ways of getting even.

Discuss how **counseling,** beginning with outpatient counseling, with someone **outside** the family, stops some adolescents because they can no longer manipulate the home setting and they decide to stop. Note, however, that some will make a game out of outpatient counseling, saying all the right things in the counseling session, but maintaining the same problem behaviors at home. Note that these adolescents may need more intense counseling, either in a **hospital** setting, if their behaviors become drastic (suicidal, depressed, etc.), or, in some cases, in a **residential treatment center** or live-in school. These adolescents, removed from the amenities of home, may indeed experience the absence from home as the ultimate negative consequence and decide to stop the problem behaviors.

Note, however, that some adolescents still will not "bottom out" with these consequences, and will stop only when faced with **legal** consequences and placed on probation.

Emphasize that this legal consequence, as discussed in the opening scenario of the session, may, unfortunately, be the only consequence which the adolescent may experience as truly unpleasant enough to get him or her to stop the problem behavior.

12. Discuss the SCHOOL setting, using **truancy** as an example, and go through each consequence on the continuum. Note how some adolescents may stop after **lectures** or warnings, but others, as in the case of the home setting, will need more severe consequences such as **detention.** Still others may see detention as fun (as in the movie "The Breakfast Club").

Note that some adolescents may need **suspension** as the ultimate negative consequence, while still others may see suspension as "time off" for surfing, hanging out, etc., and may require **expulsion** as the ultimate negative consequence. And still others may see expulsion as "no big deal," looking forward to a new school or a full time job. They may need **counseling** as the final consequence. Still others, as mentioned earlier, may use diversion counseling as a short delay before returning to their truant behaviors. Ultimately, some adolescents may require the legal consequences of probation as the final unpleasant consequence which will motivate them to cease their truant behaviors.

13. Discuss the COMMUNITY setting, using **shoplifting** as an example, noting how some adolescents are **one time** offenders, who stop after being warned by the store authorities or after having a "meeting" with parents and store owners.

    Note that some adolescents, however, experience the "meetings" as **fun** because of the inconvenience or embarrassment it causes their parents who have to go to the meeting with the store owners or security guards. Consequently, some adolescents require **restitution** as the ultimate negative consequence, wanting to get the incident off their record by paying the debt. Still others take restitution lightly, figuring they can pay off the debt gradually while continuing shoplifting elsewhere. Consequently, some adolescents may need **counseling** as the final consequence. Still others, as mentioned above, may use counseling as a diversion while continuing to shoplift. Ultimately, some adolescents may **only** respond to the legal consequence of **probation** as the significant negative consequence to motivate them to stop shoplifting.

14. Discuss the PROBATION setting, noting that, even when a **legal** consequence occurs for a behavior, different **levels of negativity** are experienced by adolescents within the legal system.

Explain that the first level is **informal** probation, wherein the legal consequence of probation is held over the adolescent's head. The adolescent is told that, if he or she avoids crime for the next six months, the charge will be dropped and the adolescent will be taken off informal probation. Usually, no probation officer is assigned during this time. For some adolescents, this is the ultimate humiliating experience and they stop any further illegal action. For some, however, it is a case of "out of sight, out of mind." That is, if no probation officer is assigned and no immediate legal consequence occurs, then no negative experience has been felt. Consequently, some adolescents require **formal** probation, while **living at home,** as the ultimate negative consequence, wherein they have to report to a probation officer regularly. They have a list of probation rules which, if violated, could result in spending time in Juvenile Hall. Still others, however, do not experience formal probation while living at home as negative because they realize that the probation officer has a large caseload and may not be able to keep a close watch on them. Thus, formal probation while living at home can become a "game" for some adolescents who are preoccupied with trying to "beat the system." Consequently, some adolescents require probation while **living outside the home** as the ultimate negative consequence. They live in small group homes in the community, with strict rules and curfews, and daily group meetings while attending school in the community or at a court approved school. Still others, however, see this as another game and use it as an opportunity to "test the limits" of the small group home setting. It is not experienced by some as ultimately unpleasant. These adolescents, then, require probation in a **work camp,** usually 6 months to a year. Most adolescents who reach this level of probation tend to "bottom out," experiencing the hard labor and inconvenience of a work camp as the ultimate negative consequence which will stop their illegal behaviors. And yet, some adolescents still challenge the camp setting, continuing to experience the legal consequences as "a game," and ultimately ending up in **Youth Prison,** remaining behind bars, off and on, until 18 or sometimes beyond, into adulthood.

15. Conclude this session by noting that each adolescent "bottoms out" somewhere along the continuum of negative consequences. Emphasize that many explanations can be given as to why one adolescent "bottoms out" earlier on the continuum than others, even within the same family. Emphasize that the best parents can do for their adolescents is to help them experience **consistent** consequences for their behaviors (positive and negative) so that they can make choices about whether to continue or stop their problem behaviors.

16. Introduce Session 11 by noting that parents can help themselves in setting up consequences for their adolescent's behaviors by being aware of the **developmental age** of their adolescent and by being aware of some basic **behavioral principles** associated with behavior change. Inform them that in Session 11 developmental and behavioral approaches will be considered for dealing with adolescents.

THEORIES OF ADOLESCENT BEHAVIOR

GOALS

1. To help parents and adolescents understand the theories of adolescent behavior: analytic, humanistic, biological (developmental), and behavioral.

2. To help parents understand how they can use the biological and behavioral approaches to enhance parent-adolescent interactions within the family.

INFORMATION

Session 11 is in the form of a lecture on four theoretical approaches to understanding adolescence: (1) analytic, (2) humanistic, (3) biological (developmental), and (4) behavioral. After a brief discussion of the analytic and humanistic approaches, most of the lecture centers around the biological (developmental) and behavioral theories of adolescent behaviors.

Emphasize the following points:

- The developmental age of adolescents is important in considering behavior.

- In viewing behavior, one needs to consider the extent to which the adolescent's behaviors are **habit** patterns that can be changed.

PROCEDURES

1. Direct parents and adolescents to sit together during this session.

2. Introduce the topic for the session by noting that, within the field of mental health, at least four orientations, or ways of explaining adolescent behaviors, are presently used.

3. Using the example of an adolescent showing severe explosive, destructive **temper tantrums,** briefly summarize how each of the four orientations would explain the adolescent's behavior, as provided in Procedures 4,5,6, and 7.

4. Write the word ANALYTIC on the chalkboard. Explain that the **analytic** approach towards understanding adolescence originated with Freud, who, in general, explained behaviors in terms of **unconscious conflict.** Thus, if an analytically oriented mental health professional were attempting to explain the temper tantrums, he or she would look for an underlying unconscious conflict, probably in early childhood, which the temper tantrum represents. Explain that treatment in this orientation is usually long-term and on-going.

5. Write the word HUMANISTIC on the chalkboard. Explain that the **humanistic** approach is based upon the presumption that every human being is potentially healthy, and simply experiences obstacles to realizing his or her potentially healthy growth. In the context of an adolescent with temper tantrums, the humanistic mental health professional might tend to cite **blocked feelings** or blocked awareness of feelings as an obstacle to growth.

   Explain that the humanistic approach emphasizes the importance of awareness of the **polarities** of **feelings** as a way of developing full growth, in contrast to just perseverating on a particular end of the spectrum of feelings. Thus, the adolescent with temper tantrums would be seen as one who needs to deal with his or her temper tantrums by exploring other possible feelings which he or she may be experiencing other than the apparent anger.

Explain that the humanistic mental professional would work with the adolescent to become aware of other feelings besides anger, such as hurt, sadness, joy, etc. in order to remove the obstacle of blocked awareness of feelings and resume the process of growth as a fully human person.

6. Write the word BIOLOGICAL on the chalkboard. Explain that, more and more, the **biological** approach to understanding human behavior is gaining acceptance and exposure in the field of mental health.

Explain that the biologically oriented mental health professional would view the temper tantrums in the adolescent as being somehow linked to a **biochemical imbalance** in the brain, or some form of **neurodevelopmental** problem.

Explain that the continued research on **neurotransmitters** in the brain is helping explain the biological nature of temper tantrums, depression, mood swings, etc.

Briefly discuss how research continues to look at blood sugar, diet, genes, brain waves, and **central nervous system delays** in an effort to understand the biological explanation of human behavior.

Discuss how medications are proving effective in reducing symptoms of depression, anxiety, and even concentration difficulties.

Explain that, in most hospital settings, the biological approach is used first, to make sure there is no biochemical or biological imbalance or possible delay in the development of brain activity.

7. Write the word BEHAVIORAL on the chalkboard. Explain that the **behaviorally** oriented mental health professional would view the adolescent temper tantrums, after making sure that no biological reason exists for the tantrums, as a **habit** which probably developed as a way of dealing with frustration or limits. The behavioral mental health professional would use principles of **learning** to explain that the adolescent probably used temper tantrums as a child and learned to use tantrums as a way of getting his or her way.

    Explain that the behavioral approach attempts to teach new, more appropriate **habits** to replace the habits which are self-defeating for the adolescent.

8. Explain to parents that, in the context of trying to understand and interact with their adolescents in the family setting, they can't be expected to function as mental health professionals.

    Explain that using analytic and humanistic techniques is in the realm of the mental health therapist.

    Explain that, as parents, they certainly can make use of the biological and behavioral approaches toward dealing with their adolescents.

9. Explain that you are going to show parents how they, as parents, can use the biological and behavioral approaches to better understand possible problems which might arise when trying to interact with adolescents.

10. Erase the board. Rewrite the word BIOLOGICAL on the chalkboard. Discuss the importance of knowing the biological, developmental age of each child when parents interact with them. Explain that, although an adolescent may be 15 years old, the developmental age may be younger in some areas. That is, just as children vary in the age at which they reach the basic developmental milestones of walking and talking, so, too, may be the case in other areas of development, especially in areas connected with the development of the **central nervous system.**

Emphasize that you are going to discuss certain areas of **developmental delays** in the central nervous system which are sometimes found in adolescents having "problems."

Emphasize that not all "problem" adolescents have all the delays you are going to discuss, but an important point for parents is to be aware of these possible delays.

11. Direct all participants' attention to Form 24, *"Sample Profile of an Acting-out Adolescent"* (copy is in *Participant Workbook*).

12. Explain that, upon diagnostic evaluation, some adolescents are found to have **neurodevelopmental deficits,** either currently active, or in the recent past. Explain that the deficits are often in the form of central nervous system delays with concomitant impulsive, explosive, perseverative, random behavior patterns.

13. Write the word SEQUENCING on the chalkboard. Discuss how some adolescents have difficulty developing the skill of **sequential problem solving.** That is, they have difficulty seeing events in terms of a "beginning, middle, and end." They cannot grasp the idea that, in order to get to point "c," they have to first start at point "a," then proceed to point "b" and ultimately to point "c" (a-b-c). Explain that some adolescents simply try to jump **immediately** to point "c," and get very frustrated when they don't get there!

Explain how, usually by the sixth grade, the **central nervous system** has developed to the point where the brain can process things in a **sequence.** However, in some cases a delay occurs, and some adolescents well beyond the sixth grade still have difficulty seeing, hearing, or solving problems in a logical sequence.

Emphasize that this is a **developmental delay** which, in most cases, "catches up" by the time the adolescent turns 18 or 19. However, in the mean time, the teenager struggles with sequencing. **Consequences** for his or her actions continue to be a problem because the adolescent has difficulty **"thinking ahead"** to the logical sequential consequences for his or her behaviors.

Emphasize how some parents find themselves wondering why their adolescent keeps repeating certain behaviors, **regardless of consequences.** Explain that, for some adolescents, because of the delay in sequencing, consequences have to be repeated over and over before they "sink in."

14. Write the words VERBAL EXPRESSION on the chalkboard. Emphasize that, in some adolescents, a delay in the development of the nervous system occurs such that the adolescent has difficulty **verbally expressing** his or her feelings, ideas, or opinions accurately. Consequently, his or her **actions** end up speaking much louder than his or her words. Anger gets expressed through temper tantrums or obscenities. Hurt, sadness, and other feelings seldom get expressed. Frustration sets in, and the adolescent still can't get his or her point across. What is often taken for refusal to communicate may sometimes be lack of skill in communicating due to a **developmental delay.**

15. Write the words SOCIAL JUDGMENT on the chalkboard. Explain that one of the things that separates humans from primates is the ability to **empathize,** to "get into the other person's shoes," to show concern for others.

Explain that the frontal lobe of the brain may sometimes show a delay in development in some adolescents. Emphasize that, more than likely, the ability to empathize will eventually develop, but, in the meantime, during the adolescent years, some adolescents may appear cruel and heartless.

16. Direct participants' attention to Form 24, "Sample Profile of an Acting-out Adolescent," referred to earlier in the session, and direct them to the items listed under **"emotional correlates."**

Briefly discuss how these emotional correlates often coexist with the sequencing, verbal expression, and social judgment deficits, and are tied in with them, as noted in procedures 17 and 18.

17. Write the words "LOW TOLERANCE OF FRUSTRATION, IMPULSIVITY, and EXPLOSIVENESS on the chalkboard.

    Explain how low tolerance of frustration, impulsivity, and explosiveness are often connected with **sequencing and verbal expression deficits.** That is, the adolescent who has difficulty anticipating or accepting consequences for behaviors and who also has difficulty solving problems verbally, will often tend to be **action oriented.** Consequently, if a problem arises or a difficulty is experienced, this type of adolescent will tend to act on impulse rather than thinking ahead. He or she will tend to explode emotionally rather than verbally discuss a problem, and will want immediate removal of any frustrating situation due to a lack of long-term planning.

18. Write the words EGOCENTRICITY and ALL OR NONE on the chalkboard. Explain how egocentricity and the "all or none" syndrome are often connected to the **social judgment deficit.** That is, the egocentricity and apparent lack of concern for anyone else may often be a function of a delay in the ability to "get into another person's shoes." Thus, when an adolescent acts as if he or she has no social conscience, it may be due to biological delay rather than a personality trait.

    Explain how the "all or none" syndrome may be the most devastating emotional characteristic of all. Discuss how, for some adolescents who lack social judgment, an attitude exists of "I want it my way or no way at all."

    Tell the story of the little 6-year-old boy whom his parents nicknamed the **"double dipper"** because of the following incident. One day, when the parents took the boy and two of his friends for an ice cream cone, each child was told to pick one dip of his favorite flavor. The other two boys did so readily. However, their son said, "I want two dips." He was told he could have only one dip. He continued to perseverate on his desire for two dips, and ultimately said, "If I can't have two dips, I don't want any at all!" He ended up with *no* ice cream. As they left the store, while his two friends were enjoying their ice cream, he smiled and triumphantly said, "I won!"

Emphasize that some adolescents, because of their limited problem-solving skills and their difficulties mentioned above, become so **myopic** that they throw **everything** away if things don't go their way.

19. Erase the chalkboard, and write the words BEHAVIORAL APPROACH on the board. Emphasize that, since the delays mentioned have to do with **skill deficits,** a behavioral approach can be used to teach new skills and new habits.

    Explain that, even if no sign of developmental delay in the adolescent exists any longer, some old **habits** may still remain.

20. Direct participants to Form 25, "Treating the Deficit" (copy is in *Participant Workbook*).

21. Go through each deficit (as provided in Procedures 22 through 26) discussing how, with the use of a behavioral approach, new skills can be taught.

22. Teach, if time permits, **sequencing** through exercises in **active listening** wherein the adolescent has to listen to a series of **oral instructions** and repeat them in the order presented. **Reading** exercises are also available to teach how to **draw conclusions** in a logical sequence from visual material which is read.

23. Explain how setting up a structured program at home whereby the adolescent has to "earn" privileges enables parents to "teach" their adolescent basic **sequencing skills.** Explain how parents can teach the adolescent to **think ahead** by setting up a simple program at home whereby

appropriate behaviors are rewarded with positive consequences.

24. As for the emotional correlates to **sequencing problems** (low tolerance of frustration, impulsivity, exposivity), encourage parents to promote self-control in the adolescent through behavioral **self-management techniques** such as **relaxation** and **biofeedback.** Remind them that the home behavior contract, with an emphasis upon "earning," also encourages the adolescent to develop self-control.

25. Concerning **verbal expression deficits,** emphasize the importance of verbal **communication at home** to give the adolescent the opportunity to express his or her feelings appropriately. Remind participants of the activities in communication practiced in Sessions 6, 7, 8, and 9.

26. For **social judgment deficits,** encourage participants to practice the **empathy** exercises from Session 9.

27. End the session with a reminder to parents to be aware of the **developmental level** of their adolescent.

28. Introduce the next session by explaining that, now that parents understand the importance of using a behavioral approach to teach skills to the adolescent, the next few sessions will deal with the specifics of setting up a behavioral program at home, so that both parents and adolescents can help each other develop skills which will enhance family living.

    Explain the importance for family members to specify the **behaviors** they expect from each other, and to specify **consequences** connected with those behaviors.

29. Introduce the topic **"applying consequences"** as the topic for the next session.

PARENTAL ROLE
IN APPLYING
CONSEQUENCES

GOALS

1. To help parents and adolescents understand the importance of a structured home setting offering adolescents the opportunity to learn to **accept** and **anticipate consequences** for their behavior.

2. To help parents become effective in teaching adolescents to be responsible for their behaviors.

INFORMATION

Session 12 offers **five basic steps** for parents to raise responsible teens. The session emphasizes that, within the family setting, since consequences play such an important part in determining whether behaviors will increase or decrease, one of the main duties of parents of adolescents is to attempt to establish an atmosphere at home whereby the ádolescent receives **positive consequences** for **positive behaviors** and **negative consequences** for **negative behaviors.**

Emphasize the following points:

- The parents' role is that of helping an adolescent learn basic facts about having to "earn" his or her way in the world.

- Parents are often the only **limit setters** in today's environment of permissiveness towards adolescents.

- Often, parents are the only ones who have the thankless task of being the ones saying "no" and applying negative consequences for negative behaviors.

- The five steps involved in effectively aligning consequences with behaviors in the home setting can help an adolescent become more and more responsible.

PROCEDURES

1. Parents and adolescents are initially seated apart from each other on opposite sides of the room.

2. Introduce the session by proposing the following to the parents:

   "Imagine someone asking your son/daughter at age 25, 'What was the *one* main thing you learned from your parents during adolescence?'. What would you, as parents, like your son or daughter to say?"

3. Have parents respond aloud and you write the responses on the chalkboard (i.e., honesty, love, caring, etc.). Allow five minutes.

4. Write the word RESPONSIBLE on the chalkboard. Ask parents if they would like to be able to say that the one thing they taught their adolescent was how to be **responsible.**

5. Write the definition of responsible on the chalkboard:

   ACCOUNTABLE; LIABLE; ABLE TO ACCEPT CON-SEQUENCES FOR ONE'S OWN BEHAVIOR.

6. Direct participants' attention to Form 26, "Five Basic Steps for Parents to Help Adolescents Associate Consequences with Behaviors," (copy is in the *Participant*

Workbook) which lists five steps towards helping adolescents learn to accept consequences for their behaviors by helping them associate consequences with behaviors. Form 26 in *Participant Workbook* is same as Figure 7 in *Leader Manual.*

7. Go over *each* of the five basic steps, using the *cartoons* which are used to illustrate each step. The basic information is provided in Procedures 8 through 24.

8. Call participants' attention to **Cartoon 1** found under the heading BE CONSISTENT (copy is in *Participant Workbook*). The cartoon depicts a mother at a grocery store with her children repeatedly asking for candy. After a number of refusals, she finally "gives in" and gives them some candy. The cartoon closes with mother saying "Sometimes it's a toss up between being **consistent** or remaining **sane.**"

9. Discuss how difficult remaining consistent in the family setting really is. Discuss the different types of inconsistency: (1) **not following through** with promises or threats; or (2) not presenting a **"united front"** (i.e., as when mom disagrees with dad on whether a consequence should be applied; or when mom and dad agree and follow through, but relatives disagree and do not apply the same consequence).

   Emphasize that the **inconsistent application** of consequences for behaviors is one way of training an adolescent to become **manipulative.** That is, the adolescent will attempt to play one parent against the other in an effort to get what she or he wants, hoping that the parents will be inconsistent in carrying through with consequences for negative behaviors.

10. Ask adolescents to write onto Form 27, "Examples of Inconsistency Experienced Within the Family," (i.e., mom vs. dad; mom and dad agreed, but didn't follow through with a previously agreed upon negative consequence

(Continued on Page 95)

RAISING RESPONSIBLE KIDS:
FIVE BASIC STEPS

1. BE CONSISTENT

2. SAY WHAT YOU MEAN
MEAN WHAT YOU SAY

3. DON'T RESCUE

4. DON'T GIVE IN

5. LOOK FOR THE POSITIVES

Figure 7. Five basic steps for parents to help adolescents associate consequences with behaviors.

(grounding?) or a positive consequence (concert?). Ask the parents to write any instances of inconsistency which they can recall.

Instruct participants to write their examples onto Form 27. Emphasize that this is not a faultfinding activity, but merely a way of recognizing that, as humans, we have some difficulty remaining consistent. Ask participants to "hold on" to their responses for comparison later on in the session. Allow 5 minutes for the task. (**NOTE:** Mom and dad work together on this task. The adolescents work independently.)

11. Call the participants' attention to **Cartoon 2** with two cartoons under the heading SAY WHAT YOU MEAN, AND MEAN WHAT YOU SAY (copy is in *Participant Workbook*). One cartoon depicts parents in a car, repeatedly warning their children, making repeated "idle threats," and wondering why their children don't realize that they **mean what they say!** The second cartoon depicts Dennis pointing out to his mom that she already **told** him for the **last time** to eat his carrots!

12. Discuss with parents and adolescents the importance of SAYING WHAT YOU MEAN, by being specific with regard to expected behaviors and consequences. Emphasize that it is very important that the adolescent understands exactly what a consequence will be for a behavior.

13. Write the word GROUNDING on the chalkboard. Ask the adolescents to describe what they think "grounding" means (i.e., no phone, no TV, no stereo, no friends over, early bedtime, one week, one month, etc.). Write the responses on the chalkboard. Usually a variance is present within the group. Emphasize that each family may differ, but they need to be **specific** and **realistic** when they spell out the expectations and conditions at home.

14. Write the words HOME BY TEN on the board. Ask parents what they mean by "home" (i.e., in the house, on the porch, on the street, in the neighborhood, etc.). Write the responses on the chalkboard. Ask the parents what

"ten" means (i.e., exactly 10, 10:05, 10:15, etc.). Write the responses on the chalkboard. Usually variance is present within the group. Once again remind the parents to be specific in their own family discussions.

15. Discuss with parents and adolescents the importance of MEANING WHAT YOU SAY. Emphasize that parents need to make sure that, whatever they promise as a positive consequence, or delineate as a logical negative consequence, they **deliver** it.

    Emphasize that whatever specific consequences are delineated, they need to be carried out (i.e., grounding, loss of car, loss of TV or stereo, loss of phone, etc.) according to the **designated** length of time or specific conditions agreed upon **prior** to the behavior which led to the consequence.

    Emphasize, that, if the parents back off from the consequence, the adolescent quickly realizes that the parents do not mean what they say, and this often leads to increased testing of the limits by the adolescent.

16. Call participants' attention to **Cartoon 3** under the heading DON'T RESCUE (copy is in *Participant Workbook*). The cartoon depicts a mother scolding her young son for scribbling on the wall with a crayon. Grandma enters the scene, defends the child, and blames mother for being too harsh. The comic strip ends with the child in grandma's arms, saying to himself, "With grandmas you're **innocent even when proven guilty!**"

17. Define "rescuing" as letting someone "off the hook" after catching them in the act, when there was an agreed upon negative consequence for the negative behavior. Briefly discuss the stereotype of grandparents who are seen as "rescuers" in their grandchildrens' eyes.

18. Discuss the natural tendency in parents to "rescue" their child from harmful consequences. Discuss the natural parental tendency to "rescue" a child from accusations

by teachers in kindergarten or early school years, with the remark, "Not my kid!"

Discuss the need for parents to "let go" and allow their adolescent to "face the music" of negative consequences.

Discuss briefly how, at times, it may even be necessary, as was discussed in Session 10, to allow the adolescent to experience **legal** consequences for illegal behaviors in order to learn a lesson.

19. Ask the adolescents to write memories of times when they were "caught" by their parents, but, for one reason or another, they were "let off the hook." Ask the parents to write incidents where they remember "rescuing" their child, for whatever reason. Ask them to write their responses on Form 28, "Examples of Rescuing or Being Rescued." Allow five minutes.

    Once again, remind them that this is not a faultfinding exercise, but an awareness exercise, reminding us of our natural tendencies. Instruct them to "hold on" to their responses for comparison later on in the session.

20. Direct participants' attention to **Cartoon 4** with two cartoons under the heading DON'T GIVE IN (copy is in *Participant Workbook*). The top comic strip portrays a camp psychologist talking to a young camper about changing times. The child responds by saying, "I believe in the old values . . . scream your head off and they'll (parents will) give in."

21. Discuss how adolescents, over the years, learn lots of ways to "scream their heads off" (i.e., temper tantrums, running away, threats, suicidal gestures, etc.) in the hope of getting their parents to "give in" and remove a negative consequence.

22. Explain that "giving in" increases the likelihood that the negative behaviors will continue. Relate the psychology experiment in **learning** as follows:

If a pigeon receives a kernel of corn every time it pecks on a lever, it will continue pecking as long as the corn is delivered. If, after a while, the corn is no longer delivered, the pigeon will eventually stop pecking and lose interest in the lever. However, if, after the corn is initially no longer delivered, a kernel of corn is delivered **every once in a while** as the pigeon pecks on the lever, the pigeon will continue to peck **indefinitely,** expecting another kernel of corn with the next peck.

Explain that every time parents "give in" after a negative behavior from their adolescent, it's like the kernel of corn which comes **every once in a while.** And, just like the pigeon, the adolescent may **continue** the negative behavior, expecting the parents to "give in" the next time a negative behavior occurs, figuring, "they gave in once, maybe they'll give in again!"

23. The second cartoon on the page has a mother saying to her child "It's time you learn that NO is a complete sentence!".

    Ask the adolescents whether they accept the first "no" as definitive, or as a challenge to change the "no" into a "yes" or at least into a "maybe." Ask the parents whether their initial "no" is definitive.

24. Direct participants' attention to **Cartoon 5** under the heading LOOK FOR THE POSITIVES. The comic strip from Andy Capp depicts Flo attempting to make peace with her husband, vowing not to nag him and to find something **positive** to say to him. As she walks in the door, she finds that the room is a mess, with papers, beverage cans, and food strewn throughout the room and on the couch where he is lying. As she walks into the room, she pauses, looks up and says, "You've certainly kept the *ceiling* nice an' tidy."

    Emphasize that, within the family, especially during teenage years, it is **imperative** to look for **positives** and to catch the adolescent "being good" with enthusiastic, animated reactions to positive behaviors.

Emphasize that during the adolescent years, inevitably, negative interactions will occur as the teenager struggles for independence and tries on new behavior and limit testing. However, if the emphasis is upon **positives,** the negatives become more bearable.

Emphasize that a "four-to-one" ratio of **positives** to **negatives** should occur in the average healthy relationship. Thus, for every negative interaction between parent and adolescent four positive interactions should take place. Encourage families to aim for this ratio as a goal, calling their attention to Form 29, "86 Ways to Say 'Very Good'," (copy is in *Participant Workbook*).

25. Instruct participants to sit *together* as families and *briefly* compare notes on the "inconsistency" (Form 27) and "rescuing" episodes (Form 28) which they completed earlier in the session. Allow five minutes.

26. Conclude the session by encouraging parents and adolescents to concentrate on the five basic steps (Form 26 in *Participant Workbook*, the same as Figure 7 in the *Leader Manual*) while setting up a system for applying consequences.

27. Introduce the 13th session by noting that, in *applying negative consequences*, an important point is to distinguish between *punishment*, which has a "gotcha" mentality, and the calm application of *logical and natural consequences* for behaviors.

Explain that Session 13 will offer an opportunity for families to learn to distinguish punishment from logical consequences, and to assess how consequences are handed out in their own family setting.

PUNISHMENT VERSUS LOGICAL AND NATURAL CONSEQUENCES

PARENTAL ASSESSMENT

GOALS

1. To help parents and adolescents understand the difference between punishment and the use of logical and natural consequences for negative behavior.

2. To help parents and adolescents **assess** whether, at present, consequences at home are being applied as punishment or as logical and natural consequences.

INFORMATION

Session 13 centers around the topic of how to apply **negative consequences** in the home setting.

Emphasize the following points:

- Often, parents and adolescents get caught up in negative interactions and power struggles.

- Parents need to distinguish between the two ways of applying negative consequences for negative behavior—

  1. PUNISHMENT, which is an after-the-fact reaction by parents to a negative behavior by the adolescent, and

  2. LOGICAL AND NATURAL CONSEQUENCES, which are an **anticipated** result of specified behaviors.

- Punishment is usually done in a **hostile fashion,** sometimes with **physical components,** often in a random fashion, often with yelling and screaming, and often with much more severity than the behavior itself warrants. It usually occurs in the context of "gotcha!". That is, the parent is often upset at the occurrence of a specific behavior, and then decides to "pour it on."

- The **logical and natural consequence,** in contrast to punishment, is presented in a **calm, rational** manner, with no hostility and no physical components. It is consistently applied based upon previously discussed agreement between the parent and the adolescent with the consequence being proportionate to the behavior. Logical consequences, then, are designed to match the needs of a particular situation.

  Logical consequences are best when set up in **advance** so that the adolescent knows what to expect.

- Finally, the **dangers** of punishment (i.e., alienation, continued opposition, etc.) and the **benefits** of logical and natural consequences (i.e., the child eventually takes responsibility for his or her own behaviors) should be stressed.

PROCEDURES

1. Direct parents and adolescents to sit apart from each other, on opposite sides of the room.

2. Introduce the session by noting that one of the most difficult tasks in a household with an adolescent is applying a negative consequence for a negative behavior.

3. Direct participants' attention to Form 30, "How Parents Deliver Negative Consequences" (copy in *Participant Workbook*).

4. Instruct **parents** to fill out Form 30, rating themselves on their attitude and approach in applying negative consequences (i.e., Is it in retaliation? Is it reasonable? Are the consequences given calmly? Are the consequences arbitrary? Are they appropriate to the problem behavior?). Mom and dad rate themselves **separately.**

5. Instruct **adolescents,** at the same time, to rate their parents (mom and dad separately). Allow 5 minutes.

6. Introduce the topic of **punishment** versus **logical** and **natural** consequences, emphasizing the points listed above under INFORMATION.

7. Remind participants that giving **positive** consequences for **positive** behaviors is also important.

8. Direct participants' attention to Form 31, "How Parents Deliver Positive Consequences" (copy is in *Participant Workbook*).

9. Direct **parents** to rate themselves on how they deliver positive consequences at home (i.e., Are the rewards meaningful? Are expected behaviors clearly stated? Do I start with small expectations? Am I enthusiastic when rewarding? Do I follow through with rewards?). Have mom and dad complete this section *separately.* Emphasize that *positive* consequences are even more important than negative consequences.

10. Direct **adolescents,** at the same time, to rate their parents (individually) on the same items (i.e., Do the rewards mean a lot? Are the behaviors clearly stated? etc.).

11. Allow five minutes for the task.

12. Direct participants' attention to Form 32, "Parental Resources for Consequences" (copy is in *Participant Workbook*).

13. Ask **parents (together)** to put a check next to any items which they are presently using as consequences at home.

14. At the same time, ask the **adolescent** to put a check next to any items which are presently being used as consequences at home.

15. Allow five minutes.

16. Direct adolescents and parents to **sit together** and **compare** their responses on Form 30, "How Parents Deliver Negative Consequences." Emphasize the importance of noting similarities and differences in their appraisals, **not arguing.** Allow five minutes for discussion between parents and their adolescent.

17. Briefly remind all participants that negative consequences need to be anticipated, and need to be delivered **calmly,** with as little emotional display as possible, so that the emphasis is upon the **consequence** rather than the way the consequence is delivered.

    Remind participants that, if the negative consequence is not discussed ahead of time, the adolescent will often become preoccupied with how "unfair" it is rather than seeing that he or she earned it.

18. Direct parents and adolescents to compare their responses on Form 31, "How Parents Deliver Positive Consequences." Once again emphasize the importance of noting similarities and differences in their appraisal, not arguing. Allow five minutes for discussion between parents and their adolescent.

19. Briefly remind all participants that the more they emphasize **positive consequences** at home, the easier their task will be to handle the negative consequences when they

occur. Remind them once again of the four-to-one positive to negative ratio mentioned in Session 12.

20. Emphasize the importance of **enthusiasm** and **animation** when giving positive consequences so that both parents and adolescents will **remember** the positive events.

21. Direct participants to compare their responses on Form 32, "Parental Resources for Consequences." Direct them to discuss not only the items which they presently use as consequences but items which may be used in the *future.*

22. Conclude the session by reminding parents and adolescents that the purpose of completing and discussing Forms 30, 31, and 32 during the session was to emphasize the importance of **discussing** and **anticipating** behaviors and logical consequences in order to avoid a punishment scenario at home.

23. Introduce Session 14 by reminding participants of the **Law of Effect** which was discussed in Session 10. The basic concept is that behavior is a function of its consequence. Remind them that the last two sessions (Sessions 12 and 13) have dealt with CONSEQUENCES. Mention that the next session will look at the other side of the equation, BEHAVIORS.

   Instruct participants to be thinking of **specific behaviors** that they want to **increase** or **decrease** in each other.

   Emphasize that the next session will dwell on how to get **specific** when talking about what **behaviors** you expect of each other at home.

IDENTIFYING BEHAVIORS

GOALS

1. To help parents and adolescents understand the importance of being specific when it comes to discussing behaviors expected of each other.

2. To teach parents and adolescents to communicate in specific, concrete terms rather than in vague generalities.

INFORMATION

Session 14 emphasizes how family problems often arise because family members often are too **vague** with each other concerning what they expect of each other.

Emphasize the following points:

- Words are often thrown around in **ambiguous** fashion, and often, each family member has his or her own definition or perception of what those words mean.

- Just as in the previous two sessions a discussion was held as to being **specific** about what **consequences** would result from a behavior, this session stresses the importance of making sure that the expected **behavior** is spelled out **specifically.**

PROCEDURES

1. Instruct parents and adolescents to sit together.

2. Write the words TRUST, RESPECT, UNDERSTANDING, and RESPONSIBLE on the chalkboard.

3. Direct participants to Form 33, "Defining Behaviors Worksheet" (copy is in *Participant Workbook*). Ask each participant to **write** his or her own **definition** for each word.

4. Allow 10 minutes. **No discussion** is to be permitted among participants.

5. Introduce the topic of the importance of being **specific** when it comes to discussing family issues. Mention the points listed above under INFORMATION.

6. Introduce the words TRUST, RESPECT, UNDERSTANDING, and RESPONSIBLE as typical "words" which are used in family settings, and which can often lead to ambiguous interpretation and arguing.

7. Emphasize that you will go through each of the four words in an effort to develop **specific** examples of what each word means.

8. Ask each participant to read aloud his or her **definition** of the word TRUST. Begin with the adolescents, and write responses on the chalkboard.

9. Write the "dictionary" definition of the word TRUST on the chalkboard: "to **believe** in another person; to have **confidence** in another person, allowing him or her to do something **without fear** of the consequences."

10. Discuss how trust develops in parents toward their children. Ask the **adolescents** how trust **develops.** Write the responses on the chalkboard.

11. Emphasize that trust has to be earned.

12. Ask **adolescents** how they earned their **parents' trust** (emphasize that trust is earned through **action,** not through **promises**).

13. Ask **adolescents** how trust is **lost** (emphasize that trust is lost through **behavior,** and can only be **regained** through **behavior).**

14. Ask **adolescents** to list the **major areas** where most adolescents **lose** trust with their parents. Write the responses on the chalkboard.

15. Ask the parents to add to the list if the adolescents have not covered all the areas. Usually there are two major areas: (1) parents do not trust that the adolescent's **word** means anything (i.e., the adolescent doesn't mean what he or she says); and (2) parents do not trust the adolescent's **judgment** (i.e., choice of friends, saying "no" to peer pressure, etc.).

16. Ask **adolescents** how **long** they think it would (or will) take to regain their parents' trust in areas where it has been lost. Write the responses on the chalkboard.

17. Ask **parents** how **long** they think it would (or will) take to trust their adolescent after trust has been lost. Write the responses on the chalkboard.

18. Emphasize that developing trust is very difficult; however, losing it is very easy.

19. Emphasize that, if trust is lost, parents need to **delineate** for the child what **behaviors** have to occur before the trust can be regained.

20. Emphasize that, usually in the context of family arguments, the adolescent wants his or her parents to "trust" him or her **before proving** by his or her behaviors that he or she can be trusted. For example, the conversation usually goes something like: "**Trust** me, mom (dad) I can handle myself." (14 year old daughter who wants to date a 19 year old); or "I know I have a temper around

the house, but I'll be calm behind the wheel, **trust** me."
(Impulsive 16 year old with a driver's permit).

21. Emphasize that, whenever the word "trust" is introduced
    in the family, all parties must spell out what **behaviors**
    are needed to earn trust, or what behaviors lost the trust,
    and what behaviors are needed to **regain** the trust.

22. Emphasize that trust comes **after** behavior has **earned**
    it, not before!

23. Introduce the word RESPECT.

24. Ask **each** participant to read **aloud** his or her definition
    of the word. Begin with the **adolescents,** and write down
    the responses on the chalkboard.

25. Write the dictionary definition on the chalkboard: "To
    have **consideration** for another person; to hold another
    person in **esteem;** to **care** about another person."

26. Emphasize that the word "respect" is **vague,** as are the
    dictionary definition words "consideration," "esteem," and
    "caring."

27. Emphasize that when parents or adolescents say to each
    other, "I want you to show me some **respect,"** they must
    spell out what they mean.

28. Ask **adolescents** to give **specific** examples of behaviors
    by adolescents which parents would see as **disrespectful**
    (e.g., cursing, lying, sarcasm). Write the responses on
    the chalkboard.

29. Ask parents to add to the list. Write the responses on
    the chalkboard.

30. Ask **parents** to give **specific** examples of behaviors by
    parents which are **disrespectful toward adolescents**
    (e.g., repeated nagging, babying, put downs, sarcasm,
    etc.). Write the responses on the chalkboard.

31. Ask the **adolescents** to add to the list. Write the responses on the chalkboard.

32. Introduce the word UNDERSTANDING.

33. Ask **each** participant to read **aloud** his or her definition of the word. Begin with the **adolescents,** and write the responses on the chalkboard.

34. Write the dictionary definition of "understanding" on the chalkboard: "to **perceive** what is **meant.**" Explain that being able to understand is to have the ability to **"put one's self in another person's shoes."**

35. Emphasize that, often, in the context of family communications, when the adolescent says to his or her parents, "You don't **understand,"** what the adolescent really means is "You don't **agree** with me!"

36. Emphasize that parents often get involved in lengthy **discussions** with the adolescent in an effort to get the adolescent to grasp that they do, in fact, **understand** the adolescent, because "they were once young themselves, they care, etc., etc., etc." However, at the time of the discussion, what the adolescent is looking for is **not** understanding, but agreement.

37. Give the following example:

    A father tells his 16 year old son that he wants him home by **midnight,** and the boy says, "Dad, you don't understand! It's embarrassing. I have to ask the guys to drop me off when they're staying out. They call me names and make fun of me for being 'daddy's little boy.' " Dad then responds by saying, "Son, I know. I've been there, I had to go through the same embarrassment when I was your age. But I just feel very strongly about this, and I want you home by midnight." The boy then says, "Dad, you just don't understand!" Dad then **continues** the discussion, trying to **assure** his son that he does, indeed, understand. However, regardless of his remarks to his son, the son continues to say, "Dad, you just don't understand!" Finally, worn out by the conversation, dad gives in, and says his son can come home at 1 AM. Suddenly his son turns to him and says, "Dad, you really understand!" Translated, this means, "Dad, you finally agree with me!"

38. Emphasize that, within families, when the phrase "you don't understand" arises, it is important not to belabor the topic with whether one person actually **understands** or not. Since it is usually the adolescent saying that the parent doesn't understand, the task of the parent is simply to show the adolescent that he or she understands by **listening,** and perhaps **repeating** what the adolescent says, and then get off the topic of "understanding."

39. Introduce the word RESPONSIBLE.

40. Ask the participants to read aloud their definitions of the word. Begin with the **adolescents,** and write the responses on the chalkboard.

41. Write the dictionary definition on the chalkboard: "To be **liable,** to be **accountable."**

42. Emphasize that responsible means **liability,** not **reliability.** Emphasize that often, within families, "when are you going to become responsible?" often means "when are you going to become reliable?"

43. Discuss becoming responsible in terms of learning to **accept consequences for one's behavior.** Emphasize that a responsible adolescent is one who is **accountable** for his or her behavior, positive or negative. A responsible adolescent takes pride in his or her positive behaviors, acknowledging compliments and praise without "undoing" them. A responsible adolescent also sticks to his or her word and accepts negative consequences without overreacting and making things worse.

Emphasize that parents can watch their adolescent become more and more responsible as he or she learns to accept consequences for his or her behavior rather than attempting to blame others, or parents.

44. Emphasize that responsibility comes with **maturity** over **time.**

45. Conclude the session by reminding the participants that, just as they worked during this session to come up with specific examples in connection with the four vague words of TRUST, RESPECT, UNDERSTANDING, and RESPON-SIBLE, the important point for them in the future is to get specific in all areas of communication which appear vague when discussing family issues.

46. Introduce Session 15 by noting that, having discussed **consequences** and **behaviors** in the past few sessions, the next session will involve an activity in **family contracting,** wherein parents and adolescents list specific **behaviors** which they expect of each other, and specific consequences which will be connected with those behaviors. Doing so is an activity of **mutual compromise** in an effort to promote **positive** interactions among family members.

DEVELOPING A FAMILY BEHAVIOR CONTRACT

GOALS

1. To give parents and adolescents an opportunity to practice how to negotiate and "contract" with each other in an effort to promote **positive** behaviors toward each other.

2. To review a sample "seven step" contracting activity with parents and adolescents.

INFORMATION

The use of mutual **contracting** is introduced as one way of solving problems which may arise between parents and adolescents.

Contracting is an approach whereby the parents and adolescents acknowledge that problems often do exist within the family and **both** parents and adolescents can attempt to solve problems by deciding to **cooperate.**

Emphasize the following points:

- Contracting is not a "cure-all," but merely an attempt to increase **positive** interactions. Thus, when the inevitable negative interactions occur, they are seen in the context of an overall **positive** atmosphere in the family.

- Mutual contracting presumes **responsibility** on the part of both parents and adolescents, **each** acknowledging that he or she may be part of the problem.

- The specific activity practiced during this session presumes **maturity** which may or may not be present in participants.

- This session is meant merely to give participants an opportunity to "get a feel" for a mutual contracting problem-solving approach.

- Each step in this contracting activity may take **days** or even **weeks** to perform and complete.

- All steps will be practiced during this one session in order to allow participants to sample **all** parts of a contracting activity in one session.

PROCEDURES

1. Direct parents and adolescents to sit together.

2. Introduce the topic of contracting, noting the points listed earlier under "Information."

3. Direct participants' attention to Form 34, "Family Behavior Contracting" (copy is in *Participant Workbook*).

4. Review those items on the top of Form 34 as follows.

5. Emphasize once again that the purpose of the contract is to increase **positive** interactions.

Emphasize that all behavior discussed in the contract should be worded **positively,** not negatively.

Emphasize that the contract should **not** list **negative** threats (e.g., if you don't go to school, you'll be grounded for two weeks). Rather, it should list **positive** rewards (e.g., if you go to school all week, you can go out on weekends).

6. Emphasize that all behaviors on the contract need to be **specific,** not general. Emphasize that the items should be described so that you could take a picture of each item as it occurred.

   Thus, specify whether "be home by 10 PM" means in the **house,** on the **front porch,** in the **neighborhood,** etc. Specify whether 10 PM means exactly 10:00, or 10:05, or 10:10, etc.

7. Emphasize that all behaviors on the contract need to be **realistic.**

   Thus, **parents** should not expect a mature 17-year-old boy to be home "when it gets dark." Moreover, if an adolescent has been having difficulty with math over the years, parents should not expect an "A" in trigonometry just because dad got one when he was young. Likewise, **adolescents** need to be realistic in their expectations of their parents' behaviors. A 13-year-old should not expect his or her parents to give him or her a 2 AM curfew on weekends.

8. Emphasize that **empathy** is the most important part of making a contract work. That is, a very important procedure is for parents and adolescents to "get into each other's shoes" when it comes to appreciating how much effort goes into the various behaviors listed on the contract.

   Emphasize that, if an adolescent with a long history of truancy starts going to school every day as part of the contract, **parents** need to grasp how **difficult** that is for the **adolescent.** And, if a parent agrees to let the adolescent get a driver's license and use the family car, the **adolescent** needs to appreciate how **difficult** this may be for the **parents** (e.g., insurance, worry about accidents, etc.).

9. Direct participants' attention to the "Activity" part of Form 34, which spells out activities and seven (7) steps of making the contract. Briefly review the seven (7) steps (listed in parentheses). Write them on the chalkboard.

   (1) Identifying **rewards** which **you can offer** the other family member(s);

   (2) Identifying **rewards** which **you want** from the other family member(s);

   (3) Setting **priorities** on the rewards you want;

   (4) Setting the **costs** on the rewards you will offer the other family member(s);

   (5) Making sure all items are **specific** and **realistic;**

   (6) **Empathizing** with each other;

   (7) Trading off rewards—**negotiating** rewards with each other.

10. Direct participants' attention to Forms 35 and 36, (copies are in *Participant Workbook*). Make sure that **parents** have Form 35, "Parent Catalog Cards: Reinforcers for Teens," and that **adolescents** have Form 36, "Teen Catalog Cards: Reinforcers for Parents." Have both parents work **together** on the same Parent Catalog Card sheet.

11. Introduce Step 1 of the contract, "Identifying rewards for others," Form 34.

    Emphasize that this first step involves trying to list what you think the other person **would like from you.** That is, parents try to figure out which behaviors on Form 35 their adolescent would most like for them to do, and the adolescent tries to figure out which behaviors on Form 36 his or her parent would most like for him or her to do.

12. Direct participants to look at the items listed on Forms 35 and 36, Parent and Teen *"Catalog Cards."* Emphasize that these are items which, in the past, other families have listed as possible behavior areas which could be used as **rewards** for each other.

13. Direct **parents** to review the 11 items listed on Form 35, "Parent Catalog Cards," beginning with "Stop nagging your adolescent about . . .," choosing 3 items on the sheet which they feel their adolescent would most appreciate. Instruct them to fill in all blank spaces and to be **specific.**

    Call their attention to the blank #12 in case they wish to write in any item or items.

    Emphasize that they must choose three (no more, no less) items.

    Remind parents to work as a **team** so they can arrive at a common estimation of the reward items which they feel their adolescent would like the most.

14. At the same time, direct **adolescents** to review the 16 items on Form 36, "Teen Catalog Cards" beginning with "Do . . . minutes of homework nightly . . .," choosing **three** items which they think their parents would like the most. Instruct them to pick three items (no more, no less) and to fill in the blanks with **specifics** (i.e., How many minutes of homework? Be home by what time? etc.). Call their attention to the blank #17 in case they wish to write in any item or items.

15. Allow up to five minutes for Step 1 of the activity (Procedures 11 through 14). (**NOTE:** Tell all participants to **disregard** the letters "V" and "C" until **later** in the activity.)

16. Introduce Step 2, "Identifying rewards for self," Form 34.

    Note that, while Step 1 involved trying to identify what you could do for the other family member(s), Step 2 involves taking a look at what the other person **will do for you,** and adding to the list.

17. Instruct parents and adolescents to **exchange catalog card sheets** so that **parents** have the list of things the **adolescent** will do for the parents (Form 36), and **teens** have the list of things **parents** will do for the adolescent (Form 35).

18. Instruct **parents** to review the three items which the adolescent has said he or she will do for the parents. Ask them to choose **two more** items on the adolescent catalog card, ending up with a total of five identified items. (Thus, if the adolescent has identified homework, clean room, and not talking back as three rewards for parents, the parents need to pick two more items from the list (e.g., help with chores, improve grades). Remind parents that they also may write in unlisted items.

19. At the same time, instruct **adolescents** to review the three items which their parents have said they will do for the adolescent. Ask them to choose **two more** items from the parent catalog card, ending up with a total of five items. (Thus, if the parents listed stop nagging, stop listening in on phone calls, and stop being critical of clothes as three rewards for the adolescent, the adolescent needs to pick two more items from the list (e.g., stop going through your things, let you stay out longer). Remind them that they also may write in items not on the list.

20. Allow five minutes for this step.

21. Introduce Step 3, "Setting priority on rewards," Form 34.

   Emphasize that they now have in front of them a list of five rewards, five things they would **like from each other.** That is, the parents have a list of five things they would like from their adolescent (Form 36), and the adolescent has a list of five things he or she would like from his or her parents (Form 35).

   Emphasize that their task is now to **rank** those rewards in terms of how **important** they are to them. Thus, the parents are to look at the five items they would like from the adolescent, and pick the **one** which is **most important,** marking a **"1"** next to the letter "V" on that item. Explain that "V" = **value.** Thus, the item which is **valued** the **most,** gets a **"V 1";** the item which they value second most gets a **"V 2";** 3rd most gets a **"V 3";** 4th most gets a **"V 4,"** and 5th most gets a **"V 5."** For example, if parents value "not fighting with brother/sister" the **most,** then the parents mark **"V 1"** for that item in the space provided.

22. At the same time, instruct **adolescents** to do the same thing with the 5 items which they would like from their parents, ranking each item from **"V 1** through **V 5."** Remind them that each of the five items gets a **separate** ranking. Only one item can be **"V 1,"** one **"V 2,"** one **"V 3,"** one **"V 4,"** and one **"V 5."**

23. Allow five minutes.

24. Introduce Step 4, "Setting **costs** on providing rewards," Form 34.

    Emphasize that Step 4 involves determining how **difficult** delivering the rewards listed on the sheets is actually going to be.

25. Instruct participants to **exchange sheets once again,** so that the **parents** have Form 35, "Parent Catalog Cards," and **teens** have Form 36, "Teen Catalog Cards."

    After they have made the exchange, remind them that they are now looking at a list of behaviors which they say **they will do for the other** family member(s). These are the **rewards** for the other family member(s).

26. Instruct participants to rank each of the five identified behaviors on the sheet in terms of how **difficult** it will be for them to carry out the behavior.

    Explain that the letter **"C"** on the sheet stands for **cost.** Thus, the behavior which is going to **cost** the most (not in terms of money, but in terms of energy, change in attitude, etc.), the behavior which is going to be the *most difficult to do,* gets ranked as *"C 1";* the second most difficult behavior gets ranked as *"C 2,"* and so forth. (For example, if parents feel that letting the adolescent get a driver's license is the most difficult, they mark that item *"C 1."* If an adolescent feels that no fighting with brother or sister is the most difficult, he or she marks that item *"C 1."*)

27. Allow five minutes for Step 4.

28. Introduce Step 5, "Making sure items are *realistic* and *specific,*" Form 34.

    Explain that, before a contract can be finalized, an essential procedure is for *all* items to be understood and agreed upon by all parties involved as being *specific* and *realistic.*

29. Instruct *parents* and *adolescents* to review with each other the five items on each sheet to make sure they are *specific* (How many minutes of homework? How many tardies at school? What is a clean room? etc.) and *realistic* (curfew times? allowance? etc.).

30. Allow five minutes for Step 5.

31. Emphasize that, often, in attempting to set up a contract, Step 5 takes a long time because many items may be vague or unrealistic. Emphasize that, in some cases, *immaturity* on the part of one member or another leads to an impasse, so that this contractual approach to *mutual* problem solving breaks down.

    Emphasize that, if immaturity gets in the way, and a refusal occurs on the part of both parties to arrive at a *mutual* compromise concerning what is *realistic* to expect of each other, *parents* may have to use a more *autocratic* approach, or else seek a third party counselor to facilitate the activity.

32. Introduce Step 6, *"Empathizing,"* Form 34.

Remind participants that a successful family contract depends upon how well family members try to understand each other in terms of *why* they want certain behaviors from each other, and in terms of how *difficult* certain behaviors will be for each family member.

Emphasize that, by trying to "get into each other's shoes," they can fully *appreciate* the amount of work and effort each is putting forth to fulfill the contract items.

33. Instruct parents and adolescents to go through each of the five items which are on the sheets (Forms 35 and 36), "getting into each other's shoes." Give the following instructions.

   a. *Parent* picks *adolescent's* item (Form 36) ranked *"C 1,"* and says to the adolescent (for example), "You noted that not fighting with your brother is the hardest for you. I would imagine that this is because he's always bugging you, he won't give you privacy, and he tattles on you a lot. I guess you feel you're always the one getting blamed because you're older and we 'expect' more of you."

   b. The *adolescent* then either *agrees,* or adds more reasons.

   c. The *adolescent* then picks the parents' item (on Form 35) ranked "C 1," and says to the parent(s) (for example), "You noted that letting me get a driver's license is the most difficult for you. I guess that's because you'll be worried about my being in a car with other kids. You'll probably be worried about accidents. I guess insurance is expensive, too."

   d. *Parents* then respond with *agreement* or add more reasons.

   e. Parents and adolescents continue going through each item, discussing how *difficult* each item will be. They then go through the same procedure while discussing the *importance* (value) of each of the 5 items.

34. Emphasize that **empathy** means **no lecturing.** Remind parents and adolescents that this step centers around **acknowledging** the other person's side, not disagreeing or minimizing.

35. Allow five minutes. Explain that time during the session is insufficient to complete all the items in Step 6. Explain that this session is just to give them a **sample** of each step of the activity. Encourage participants to continue this step at home.

36. Introduce Step 7, "**Trading off** rewards," Form 34.

    Explain that, presuming that all six steps had been completed fully, so that all behaviors had been fully **specified, discussed,** and **empathically understood** by all parties involved in the contract, negotiation would then take place.

37. Explain **negotiation** as a form of "let's make a deal," "you scratch my back, and I'll scratch yours," etc. Give the following examples.

    a. An adolescent wants privacy in his or her room. Mom wants the dirty clothes placed in the hallway hamper. The adolescent agrees to place all dirty laundry in the hallway hamper, and mom agrees to give the adolescent his or her privacy.

    b. An adolescent wants the family car for activities. Parents want a "C" average at school. The adolescent agrees that his or her use of the car depends upon maintaining a "C" average at school.

38. Instruct parents and adolescents to **briefly negotiate** the five items on each of their catalog card sheets (Forms 35 and 36), **trading off** one behavior for another.

39. Allow five minutes as a sample of negotiating.

40. Conclude the session by noting that the seven steps practiced during this session are just a sample of a contract approach, offered to them as a way of getting a "feel" for what it would be like to try to negotiate with each other.

41. Encourage participants to use a "negotiation" approach whenever problems arise, using all the communication skills practiced throughout the program.

42. End the session by complimenting all participants for their involvement over the several sessions of the program. Encourage them to continue to practice these activities and skills which they have learned over the 15 sessions.

BIBLIOGRAPHY

BIBLIOGRAPHY

Bean, R., and Clemes, H. (1980). *How to teach children responsibility.* Los Angeles, CA: Price, Stern, Sloan.

Becker, W. (1971). *Parents are teachers.* Champaign, IL: Research Press.

Brownstone, J., & Dye, C. (1973). *Communication workshop for parents of adolescents.* Champaign, IL: Research Press.

Burnett, D. (1982, Spring). The learning disabled delinquent: Teaching socially appropriate reactions to confrontations for negative behaviors. *Journal of Special Education Technology.* Volume V; No. 2, 44-52.

Burnett, D. (1991). *Parents, kids, and self esteem: 15 ways to help kids like themselves.* Audiotape. P.O. Box 7223, Laguna Niguel, Ca 92607-7223.

Burnett, D. (1991). *Raising responsible kids: 5 steps for parents.* Audiotape. P.O. Box 7223, Laguna Niguel, Ca 92607-7223.

Goldstein, A., Sprafkin, R., Gershaw, N., & Klein, P. (1980). *Skill-streaming the adolescent: A structured learning approach to teaching prosocial skills.* Champaign, IL: Research Press.

Growing Parent, (1985, January) Vol. 13, No. 1. Lafayette, IN 47902: Dunn and Hargitt, Inc. 22 N. Second Street.

Jensen, L., & Jensen, J. (1984). *Four principles for positive parenting.* Provo, UT: Brigham Young University.

Weathers, L., & Liberman, R.P. (1975). The family contracting exercise. *Journal of Behavior Therapy and Experimental Therapy.* 6, 208-214.

The *Ungame* Company. (1975). Anaheim, CA 92806: Post Office Box 6382.

ABOUT
THE
AUTHOR

ABOUT THE AUTHOR

Dr. Darrell Burnett, father of two teens and a pre-teen, is licensed as a clinical psychologist and as a marriage, family, and child counselor. He is credentialed as a community college teacher and counselor, and as a high school teacher and school psychologist.

He earned his Ph.D. in clinical psychology from United States International University in San Diego, California.

Following his one year Post Doctoral Fellowship in psychology at the Neuropsychiatric Institute, UCLA, Dr. Burnett has maintained an active private practice for more than 15 years in southern California working with troubled youth and families, developing programs for emotionally disturbed youth. Using his experience as a former drug counselor for the Federal Narcotic Addict Rehabilitation Program, he also develops treatment programs for chemically dependent youth.

Dr. Burnett presently consults with two psychiatric hospitals, following 12 years as Program Director of three hospital-based treatment units for youth, including a consultant contract to establish a hospital-based treatment program for youth at the Naval Base in Okinawa.

Dr. Burnett's contracts as a consultant include schools, probation departments, military bases, churches, social agencies, and business corporations.

Following 10 years as an Adjunct Professor at the Graduate School of Human Behavior, United States International University, Dr. Burnett maintains his academic interests through writing journal articles and presenting seminars and workshops on parent-child relationships, stress and anger management, teen suicide, and self-esteem, at the local, state, national, and international levels.

He maintains media involvement through TV and radio presentations.

Dr. Burnett's avocation is promoting youth sports as a positive experience. He is the author of a series of booklets on positive coaching: *The Art of Being a Successful Youth League Manager-Coach* (Funagain Press, P.O. Box 7223, Laguna Niguel, CA 92607-7223).

Dr. Burnett is presently the Director of the Responsibility Center in Orange County, California.

He is listed in the National Register of Health Providers in Psychology. He is a member of the American Psychological Association and the California State Psychological Association.